P O C K E T S
EARTH FACTS

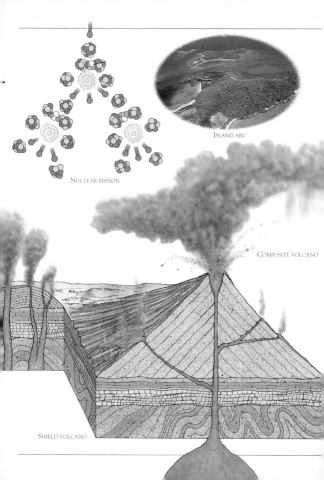

NUCLEAR FISSION

ISLAND ARC

COMPOSITE VOLCANO

SHIELD VOLCANO

P O C K E T S

EARTH FACTS

Written by
CALLY HALL and
SCARLETT O'HARA

SATELLITE PICTURE OF
EARTH'S OZONE HOLE

ONION-LAYERING

CARBONIFEROUS FOREST

DK

LONDON, NEW YORK,
MUNICH, MELBOURNE, and DELHI

Project editor Scarlett O'Hara
Art editor Susan Downing
Senior editor Laura Buller
Senior art editor Helen Senior
Editorial consultant Cally Hall
Picture research Charlotte Bush, Christine Rista
Production Louise Barratt

REVISED EDITION
Project editor Andrea Mills
Designer Darren Holt
Managing editor Linda Esposito
Managing art editor Jane Thomas
DTP designer Siu Yin Ho
Consultant Douglas G. D. Russell B.Sc. FLS
Production Erica Rosen

First published in Great Britain in 1995
by Dorling Kindersley Limited,
80 Strand, London WC2 0RL
A Penguin Company

Revised in 2004

A CIP catalogue record for this book is available from
the British Library
ISBN-13: 978-0-7566-0202-4

Colour reproduction by Colourscan, Singapore
Printed and bound in Italy by L.E.G.O.

See our complete catalogue at
www.dk.com

CONTENTS

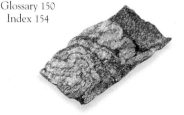

HOW TO USE THIS BOOK

These pages show you how to use *Pockets: Earth Fact*
The book is divided into 13 sections. Each section
contains information on one aspect of the Earth. The
pages in the section give further details on the topic.
At the beginning of each section there is a guide to
the contents of that section.

CORNER CODING
In the corner of
each page a colored
square indicates
the section's topic.

PLANET EARTH

EARTH'S PLATES AND
CONTINENTS

VOLCANOES

EARTHQUAKES

LANDSCAPE, WEATHER-
ING, AND EROSION

ROCKS AND MINERALS

MINERAL RESOURCES

MOUNTAINS, VALLEYS,
AND CAVES

GLACIATION

OCEANS, ISLANDS,
AND COASTS

RIVERS AND LAKES

CLIMATE AND WEATHER

A FUTURE FOR THE
EARTH

Corner coding

Heading

Introduction

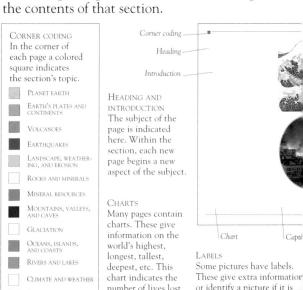

Chart

Capti

HEADING AND
INTRODUCTION
The subject of the
page is indicated
here. Within the
section, each new
page begins a new
aspect of the subject.

CHARTS
Many pages contain
charts. These give
information on the
world's highest,
longest, tallest,
deepest, etc. This
chart indicates the
number of lives lost
in several serious
earthquakes.

LABELS
Some pictures have labels.
These give extra information
or identify a picture if it is
not immediately obvious
from the text.

UNNING HEADS
s a reminder of the
ection, the left-hand
age has a running
ead with the section
ame.The running
ead of the right-hand
age gives the subject
f the particular page.

FACT BOXES
These at-a-glance
information boxes
appear on many pages.
They provide
fascinating details
about the subject.
This fact box has
details on tsunamis.

FORMATION BOXES
To explain a process, a
formation diagram may be
used. These show several
stages in a process and may
have annotation. The
diagrams and their
accompanying captions are
enclosed in a box.

Running head   *Fact box*

Formation diagram   *Map*

MAP
Some pages in the book include maps.
The world maps show where the
features discussed on the page are in
the world. Maps have annotations
and labels to aid identification and
give further information.

Label   *Annotation*

APTIONS AND ANNOTATIONS
ach illustration is accompanied
y a caption. Annotations, in
alics, point out the features of
n illustration or diagram and
sually have leader lines.

INDEX
At the back of the book, there is an
index. It lists alphabetically every subject
included in the book. By referring to the
index, information on particular topics
can be found quickly.

PLANET EARTH

HOW THE EARTH WAS FORMED

ABOUT 5 BILLION years ago our Solar System began to take shape. The Sun and the nine planets formed from a cloud of dust and gas swirling in space. Some scientists believe that the center of this cloud cooled and contracted to form the Sun. Gravity pulled the planets from the rest of the cloud. Other scientists suggest that the dust cloud formed asteroids that joined together to make the Sun and planets

1 FORMING THE SUN
A spinning cloud of gas and dust contracted to form the Sun. Cooler matter from this dust cloud combined to shape the planets.

A dense atmosphere of cosmic gases surrounded the Earth.

2 FORMING THE EARTH
The Earth's radio-activity caused the surface to melt. Lighter minerals floated to the surface and heavier elements, such as iron and nickel, sank to form the Earth's core.

3 THE EARTH'S CRUST
About 4 billion years ago, the Earth's crust began to form. Blocks of cooling, solid rock floated on a molten rock layer. The rock sometimes sank and remelted before rising again.

ARTH FACTS

The Earth orbits the
un at 18.5 miles/sec
9.8 km/sec).

Oceans cover 70.8%
the Earth's surface.

Earth is not a sphere –
bulges in the middle.

The Earth completes
turn on its axis every
hours, 56 minutes.

COMPOSITION OF
THE EARTH
The elements
here are divided
by weight. Earth's
crust consists
mostly of oxygen,
silicon, and
aluminum.
Heavier metals
such as iron and
nickel are found
in the core.

Other elements
less than 1%
Aluminum 1.1%
Sulfur 1.9%
Nickel 2.4%
Magnesium 13%
Silicon 15%
Oxygen 30%
Iron 35%

4 MAKING THE ATMOSPHERE
The Earth's crust thickened.
It took several million years
for volcanic gases to form the
atmosphere. Water vapor
condensed to make oceans.

6 THE EARTH TODAY
Earth's unique conditions are
just right to support a variety of life.
Our planet, though, continues to
change. Tectonic plates are moving,
pulling some continents nearer and
pushing others farther apart.

LAND
FORMS
out 3.5
ion years ago
tocontinents formed on the crust.
day's continents look very different.

THE EARTH IN SPACE

EARTH IS A DENSE rocky planet, third nearest to the
Sun, and tiny compared with Jupiter and Saturn.
While Earth rotates on its axis once each day, it
also orbits the Sun once each year, held in orbit
by the Sun's gravity. One moon revolves around
the Earth. From space, the Earth looks blue and
calm, but under its oceans, deep beneath the
crust, intense heat melts metal and rock.

MERCURY
• 87.96 days to orbit Sun
• diameter 3,031 miles
(4,878 km)

EARTH
• 365.26 days to orbit Sun
• diameter 7,926 miles
(12,756 km)
• 1 moon

MARS
• 686.98 days to orbit Sun
• diameter 4,217 miles
(6,786 km)
• 2 moons

VENUS
• 224.7 days to orbit Sun
• diameter 7,520 miles
(12,102 km)

SUN
• diameter 865,000 miles (1,391,980 km)

THE SOLAR SYSTEM
Our Solar System consists of nine
planets, as well as moons, asteroids,
comets, meteorites, dust, and gas. All
of these orbit a central star – the

The Great
Red Spot is a
cyclone

JUPITER
• 11.86 years to orbit Sun
• diameter 88,846 miles
(142,984 km)
• 16+ moons
• 1 ring

MERCURY   EARTH

VENUS   MARS

JUPITER

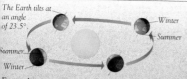

The Earth tilts at an angle of 23.5°.

Winter

Summer

Summer

Winter

EARTH'S ORBIT

As the Earth turns on its axis, it also orbits the Sun. When the Northern Hemisphere faces the Sun it has its summer. At the same time the Southern Hemisphere faces away from the Sun and has its winter. The equator faces toward the Sun most of the time and there are no significant seasonal changes there.

DISTANCE FROM THE SUN		
PLANET	MILLION MILES	MILLION KM
Mercury	36	58
Venus	67	108
Earth	93	150
Mars	142	228
Jupiter	483	778
Saturn	887	1,427
Uranus	1,784	2,871
Neptune	2,794	4,497
Pluto	3,675	5,914

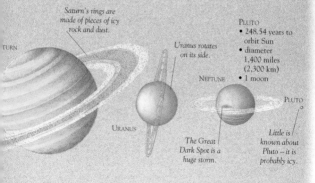

Saturn's rings are made of pieces of icy rock and dust.

Uranus rotates on its side.

NEPTUNE

PLUTO

TURN

URANUS

The Great Dark Spot is a huge storm.

PLUTO
• 248.54 years to orbit Sun
• diameter 1,400 miles (2,300 km)
• 1 moon

Little is known about Pluto -- it is probably icy.

SATURN
• 29.46 years to orbit Sun
• diameter 74,898 miles (120,536 km)
• 18+ moons
• 7 rings

URANUS
• 84 years to orbit Sun
• diameter 31,763 miles (51,118 km)
• 15+ moons
• 11 rings

NEPTUNE
• 164.79 years to orbit Sun
• diameter 30,775 miles (49,528 km)
• 8 moons
• 4 rings

EARTH'S MAGNETIC FIELD

THE EARTH BEHAVES like a giant magnet. Molten nickel and iron flowing in the molten outer core of the Earth produce an electric current. This electricity creates a magnetic field, or magnetosphere that extends into space. Like a magnet, the Earth has two magnetic poles. From time to time, the magnetic poles reverse polarity. The last time they changed was about 700,000 years ago. No one knows why this happens.

MAGNETIC POLES
North and south geographical poles lie at either end of the Earth's axis (the invisible line around which the Earth turns). The magnetic poles' position varies over time. It is the Earth's magnetic field that causes a compass needle to point north.

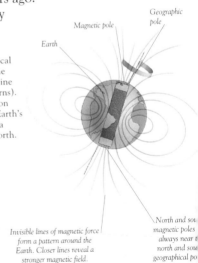

Geographic pole

Magnetic pole

Earth

Invisible lines of magnetic force form a pattern around the Earth. Closer lines reveal a stronger magnetic field.

North and sou
magnetic poles
always near t
north and sou
geographical po

MAGNETIC FACTS

• Whales and birds use the Earth's magnetic field to help them navigate.

• Every second the Sun sheds at least a million tons (tonnes) of matter into the solar wind.

GNETOSPHERE

th's magnetosphere extends
ut 37,000 miles (60,000 km)
o space. It protects the Earth
n some of the Sun's most
rmful energetic particles.

*Solar wind particles caught
by Earth's atmosphere glow
as the auroras.*

*Electrically charged particles
from the Sun push the
magnetosphere out of shape.*

*olar wind full of charged
nic particles from the Sun*

Earth

*Atomic particles are trapped
in two dense layers called
the Van Allen belts.*

*The polarity of new crust reverses
between north and south.*

MAGNETIC CRUST

New oceanic crust rises out of
the Earth at midoceanic ridges.
As the rock solidifies, a record
of the Earth's magnetism is
locked into it. Earth's
changing polarities lead to a
magnetic pattern in the rock,
symmetrical on either side of
the spreading ridge.

EARTH'S ATMOSPHERE

THE EARTH IS WRAPPED in a blanket of gases called th "atmosphere." This thin layer protects the Earth from the Sun's fierce rays and from the hostile conditions of outer space. There are five layers in the Earth's atmosphere before the air merges with outer space. The lowest layer holds air and water vapor that support life, and our weather and climate.

EXOSPHERE
- begins at 560 miles (900 km)
- thin layer before spacecra reach outer space

THERMOSPHERE
- 50–280 miles (80–450 km
- reaches 3,600°F (2,000°C)
- contains the ionosphere – electrically charged air tha reflects radio waves

MESOSPHERE
- 30–50 miles (50–80 km)
- meteors burn up and cause shooting stars

STRATOSPHERE
- 12–30 miles (20–50 km)
- ranges from -76°F (-60°C) to just about freezing poin at the top
- calm layer where airplanes fly
- contains the ozone layer that protects us from the Sun's harmful rays

TROPOSPHERE
- up to 12 miles (20 km) above the Earth
- weather layer, where rain clouds form

A THIN LAYER
The Earth's atmosphere is actually a thin blanket around the Earth. If the Earth were an orange, the atmosphere would be as thin as the skin of the orange.

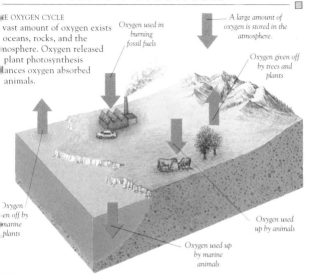

THE OXYGEN CYCLE

vast amount of oxygen exists
oceans, rocks, and the
mosphere. Oxygen released
plant photosynthesis
lances oxygen absorbed
animals.

Oxygen used in
burning
fossil fuels

A large amount of
oxygen is stored in the
atmosphere.

Oxygen given off
by trees and
plants

Oxygen
en off by
marine
plants

Oxygen used
up by animals

Oxygen used up
by marine
animals

ATMOSPHERE FACTS

The troposphere is
he densest layer of the
tmosphere.

Ozone is a type of
xygen that absorbs
amaging ultraviolet
ays from the Sun.

Humans can live and
reathe normally only
n the troposphere layer.

COMPOSITION OF THE LOWER ATMOSPHERE

Although nitrogen
makes up most of the
air we breathe, oxygen
is the essential gas for
all animal and human
life. Nitrogen is simply
breathed in and out.
Other gases, such as
argon and carbon
dioxide, make up less
than 1 percent.

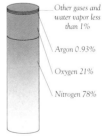

Other gases and
water vapor less
than 1%

Argon 0.93%

Oxygen 21%

Nitrogen 78%

MAPPING THE EARTH

MAPS HELP US SEE what the Earth looks like. A map uses symbols to represent different features of the Earth. A technique called "projection" can transfer t curved surface of the globe onto a flat sheet of paper. Aerial photographs help make maps that show valley and hills. On a larger sca satellite photograph help mapmaker show how th Earth looks from space

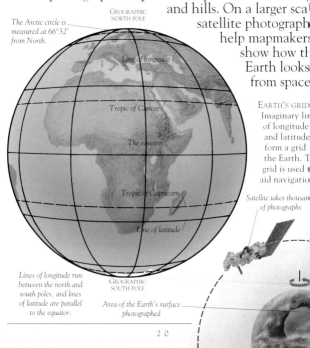

The Arctic circle is measured at 66°32' from North.

GEOGRAPHIC NORTH POLE

Line of longitude

Tropic of Cancer

The equator

Tropic of Capricorn

Line of latitude

GEOGRAPHIC SOUTH POLE

Lines of longitude run between the north and south poles, and lines of latitude are parallel to the equator.

EARTH'S GRID Imaginary lir of longitude and latitude form a grid the Earth. T grid is used aid navigatio

Satellite takes thousan of photographs

Satellite takes thousan of photographs

Area of the Earth's surface photographed

MERCATOR'S PROJECTION   PETER'S PROJECTION

MAP PROJECTIONS
Mercator's map of 1569 distorted the land area of the continents – Greenland appeared larger than Africa. Peter's map shows the right land area but the shape of the continents is incorrect.

THE WORLD'S CONTINENTS
The Earth is divided into seven land masses, or continents.

Asia is larger than Europe and Africa combined. It takes up 30% of the Earth's land.

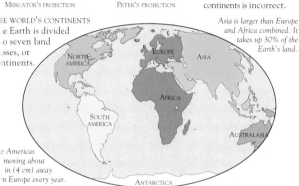

NORTH AMERICA

EUROPE

ASIA

AFRICA

SOUTH AMERICA

AUSTRALASIA

ANTARCTICA

The Americas are moving about in (4 cm) away from Europe every year.

SATELLITE MAPPING
While orbiting the Earth, satellites photograph the planet in sections. The separate images are combined to give a clear picture of the Earth.

Satellite's orbit around the poles

Direction of the Earth's rotation

THE SIZE OF THE CONTINENTS

CONTINENT	AREA IN SQ MILES	AREA IN SQ KM
Asia	17,176,100	44,485,900
Africa	11,687,180	30,269,680
North America	9,357,290	24,235,280
South America	6,880,630	17,820,770
Antarctica	5,100,020	13,209,000
Europe	4,065,940	10,530,750
Australasia	3,445,610	8,924,100

EARTH'S PLATES AND CONTINENTS

THE EARTH'S CRUST

THE EARTH'S SURFACE IS covered by a thin layer of rock called "crust." Rocky crust standing above sea level forms islands and continents. The lithosphere is in pieces, or plates, that move slowly all the time. When two plates meet they may slide past each other or one may go under another. New crust forms at ocean ridges and old crust melts into the mantle.

PLATE FACTS

• Earth's plates "float" on a layer of mantle called asthenosphere.

• The size of the Earth doesn't change – new crust produced equals older crust consumed.

EARTH'S SKIN
The Earth's crust, like the skin of an apple, is a thin covering for what is inside. Under the ocean the crust, called "oceanic crust", is 4 miles (6 km) thick, but under mountain ranges, the continental crust can be 40 miles (64 km) thick.

The rock plates the Earth's crust together like pieces of a jigsaw puzzle

CROSS SECTION OF THE EARTH'S CRUST
This section of the Earth's crust at the equator shows the landscape and the direction of plate movement at plate boundaries.

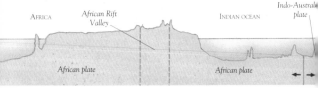

AFRICA   African Rift Valley   INDIAN OCEAN   Indo-Australian plate

African plate   African plate

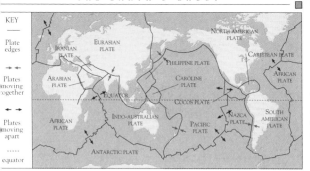

KEY

— Plate edges

Plates moving together

Plates moving apart

···· equator

PLATES OF THE WORLD
The surface of the Earth
has 15 large plates. A
plate can include both
continental lithosphere
and oceanic lithosphere.
Areas such as Australia
are in the middle of a
plate, while others, like
Iceland, have a plate
boundary through them.

MOVEMENT OF THE EARTH'S PLATES

PLATE NAMES	DIRECTION OF MOVEMENT	RATE OF MOVEMENT	
		in PER YEAR	cm PER YEAR
Pacific/Nazca	apart	7.2	18.3
Cocos/Pacific	apart	4.6	11.7
Nazca/South American	together	4.4	11.2
Pacific/Indo-	together	4.1	10.5
Pacific/Antarctic	apart	4.0	10.3

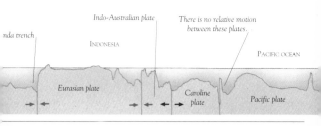

Indo-Australian plate

There is no relative motion
between these plates.

...nda trench

INDONESIA

PACIFIC OCEAN

Eurasian plate

Caroline plate

Pacific plate

MOVING CONTINENTS

EARTH'S CONTINENTS can be rearranged to fit together like pieces of a jigsaw puzzle. This idea made scientists think that they once formed a giant landmass, Pangaea. This "supercontinent" broke up and the continents drifted, over millions of years, to where they are now. This is continental drift, or plate tectonics, theory. Continents move as the Earth's plates move, sliding along on the asthenosphere, a layer of soft mantle.

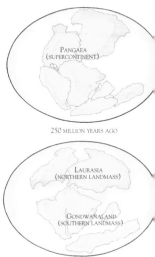

250 MILLION YEARS AGO

120 MILLION YEARS AGO

CONTINENTAL DRIFT
When Pangaea broke up, new continents emerged. The outlines of South America and Africa appeared.

CROSS SECTION OF THE EARTH'S CRUST

PACIFIC OCEAN

Pacific plate

Nazca

PLATE BOUNDARIES

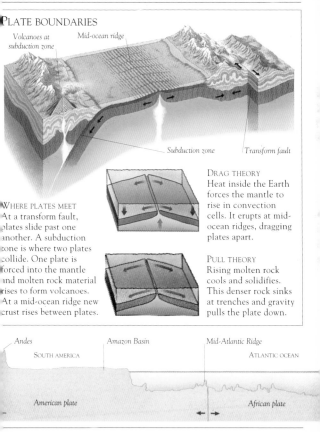

Volcanoes at subduction zone

Mid-ocean ridge

Subduction zone

Transform fault

DRAG THEORY
Heat inside the Earth forces the mantle to rise in convection cells. It erupts at mid-ocean ridges, dragging plates apart.

PULL THEORY
Rising molten rock cools and solidifies. This denser rock sinks at trenches and gravity pulls the plate down.

WHERE PLATES MEET
At a transform fault, plates slide past one another. A subduction zone is where two plates collide. One plate is forced into the mantle and molten rock material rises to form volcanoes. At a mid-ocean ridge new crust rises between plates.

Andes

Amazon Basin

Mid-Atlantic Ridge

SOUTH AMERICA

ATLANTIC OCEAN

American plate

African plate

INSIDE THE EARTH

THE INTERIOR OF the Earth has four major layers. On the outside is the crust made of familiar soil and rock. Under this is the mantle, which is solid rock with a molten layer at the top. The inside, or core, of the Earth has two sections: an outer core of thick fluid, and solid inner core

The atmosphere stretches about 400 miles (640 km) into space.

The crust varies between about 4 and 40 miles (6 and 64 km) thick.

Lithosphere

Asthenosphere

The mantle is 1,800 miles (2,900 km) thick.

The outer core is 1,240 miles (2,000 km) thick.

The inner core is 1,700 miles (2,740 km) thick.

LAYERS OF THE EARTH
Earth's outer shell is called the "lithosphere". This is t crust and part of the upper mantle. The lithosphere floats on the asthenospher like an iceberg on the sea. Earth's outer core is mostly oxygen, liquid iron, and nickel. Its inner core, abou 7,200°F (4,000°C), is solid iron and nickel.

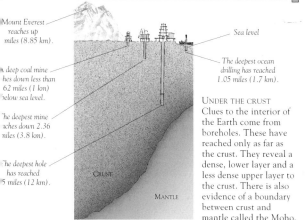

Mount Everest reaches up miles (8.85 km).

Sea level

A deep coal mine hes down less than .62 miles (1 km) below sea level.

The deepest ocean drilling has reached 1.05 miles (1.7 km).

The deepest mine aches down 2.36 niles (3.8 km).

The deepest hole has reached 5 miles (12 km).

CRUST

MANTLE

UNDER THE CRUST

Clues to the interior of the Earth come from boreholes. These have reached only as far as the crust. They reveal a dense, lower layer and a less dense upper layer to the crust. There is also evidence of a boundary between crust and mantle called the Moho.

CRUST FACTS

If an excavator could g a hole through the arth at 39 in (1 m) er minute, it would ke 24 years to reach e other side.

Western Deep Gold ine in South Africa is e world's deepest ine. It is 2.36 miles .8 km) deep.

The Earth's crust is ainly granitelike rock.

COMPOSITION OF THE EARTH'S CRUST

Light elements such as silicon, oxygen, and aluminum make up the Earth's crust. Oceanic crust is mostly basalt (which also contains magnesium and iron). Continental crust is composed of granitelike rocks. These may have formed from recycled basaltic ocean crust.

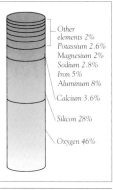

Other elements 2%
Potassium 2.6%
Magnesium 2%
Sodium 2.8%
Iron 5%
Aluminum 8%

Calcium 3.6%

Silicon 28%

Oxygen 46%

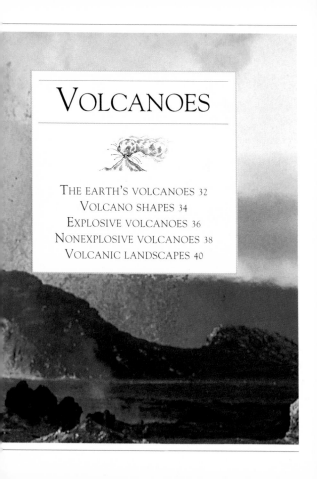

VOLCANOES

EXTINCT VOLCANO
Castle Rock, Edinburgh, is an extinct volcano. It has not erupted for 340 million years. An extinct volcano such as this is not expected to erupt again.

DORMANT VOLCANO
If scientists believe a volcano may erupt again, perhaps because it gives off volcanic gases, it is called dormant. Mt. Rainier, WA, is considered dormant.

THE EARTH'S VOLCANOES

MOST VOLCANOES are found at plate boundaries near the Pacific coast or at mid-ocean ridges. Here, fractures in the lithosphere allow molten rock, called "magma," to rise from the mantle inside the Earth. Magma is known as "lava" when it flows out of a volcano. Ash, steam, and gas also spew out from a volcano and can cause a great deal of destruction.

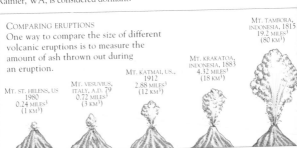

COMPARING ERUPTIONS
One way to compare the size of different volcanic eruptions is to measure the amount of ash thrown out during an eruption.

MT. ST. HELENS, US
1980
0.24 MILES^3
(1 KM^3)

MT. VESUVIUS,
ITALY, A.D. 79
0.72 MILES^3
(3 KM^3)

MT. KATMAI, US.,
1912
2.88 MILES^3
(12 KM^3)

MT. KRAKATOA,
INDONESIA, 1883
4.32 MILES^3
(18 KM^3)

MT. TAMBORA,
INDONESIA, 1815
19.2 MILES^3
(80 KM^3)

LCANO SITES

general, volcanoes, like
thquakes, occur near
te boundaries.
lcanoes are
med by plate
truction or
presence of
ot spot
lerneath
plate.

chain of volcanoes
nd the edge of the
fic Ocean is known
e "Ring of Fire."

*Ring of Fire continues
through volcanic
islands of
Japan.*

PACIFIC
OCEAN

MPEII
A.D. 79 Mt. Vesuvius erupted,
ying the town of Pompeii
der dust and ash. The two-day
ption killed 2,000 people with
sonous gases and hot ash.

LARGEST VOLCANIC EXPLOSIONS

The Volcanic Explosivity Index (V.E.I.)
grades eruptions from 0 to 8. The scale is
based on the height of the dust cloud, the
volume of tephra (debris ejected by a
volcano), and an account of the severity
of the eruption. Any eruption above 5 on
the scale is very large and violent. So far,
there has never been an eruption of 8.

VOLCANO	DATE	V.E.I.
Crater Lake, Oregon	c.4895 B.C.	7
Towada, Honshu, Japan	915	5
Oraefajokull, Iceland	1362	6
Tambora, Indonesia	1815	7
Krakatoa, Indonesia	1883	6
Santa Maria, Guatemala	1902	6
Katmai, US	1912	6
Mt. St. Helens, Washington	1980	5

VOLCANO SHAPES

NOT ALL VOLCANOES are the same. Some are cone-shaped and others are almost flat. The shape of the volcano depends on the kind of lava that erupts. Soupy, nonviscous lava spreads quickly before hardening, but stiff, viscous lava piles up near the volcanic vent. Volcanoes usually appear near plate boundaries, but they also form at hot spots such as in Hawaii. Volcanoes also exist under the ocean at plate edges.

ICELAND'S RIFT
Skaftar fissure in Iceland lies where two plates are moving apart. It is part of a 16-mile (27-km) rift along the plates' edges.

VOLCANO FACTS
• Kilauea, Hawaii, is one of the world's most active volcanoes.

• There are about 1,300 active volcanoes in the world.

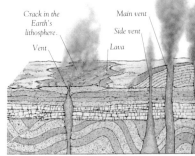

Crack in the Earth's lithosphere.

Vent

Main vent

Side vent

Lava

FISSURE VOLCANO
This type of volcano arises from a long crack in the lithosphere. Nonviscous lava flows out to form a plateau.

SHIELD VOLCANO
A large, gently slopin volcanic cone. It gro when nonviscous lav erupts from a central vent or side vents.

WORST VOLCANIC ERUPTIONS

VOLCANO	DATE	HUMAN DEATHS
Tambora	1815	92,000
Mt. Pelée	1902	40,000
Krakatoa	1883	36,000
Nevado del Ruiz	1985	23,000

COMPOSITE VOLCANO

Cone-shaped volcanoes build up from viscous lava. Inside are layers of thick lava and ash from previous eruptions. Gas pressure inside the volcano magma chamber causes violent eruptions.

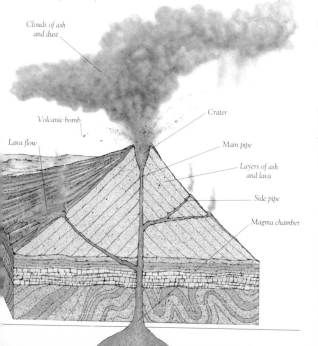

Clouds of ash and dust

Volcanic bomb

Lava flow

Crater

Main pipe

Layers of ash and lava

Side pipe

Magma chamber

EXPLOSIVE VOLCANOES

SOMETIMES VOLCANOES explode violently. Volcanoes that form from viscous lava are most likely to do this

Viscous lava tends to plug up volcanic vents. When pressure in the magma chamber increases, the lava is blown out. Pieces of rock and a great deal of ash are hurled high into the air. Clouds of ash and pumice flow like hot avalanches down the sides of the volcano. Mudflows (also called "lahars") are a mixture of water and ash. They travel at great speed and engulf everything in their paths.

NUÉE ARDENTE
An explosive eruption can cause a glowing ash cloud or *nuée ardente*.

BEFORE MT. ST. HELENS ERUPTED

MT. ST. HELENS
In the Cascades, a peaceful-looking volcano erupted after 123 years of dormancy. A warning came when one side of the volcano began to bulge as the magma rose. A gas explosion lasting 9 hours and a landslide ensued. An ash cloud over 580 miles^2 (1,500 km^2) caused darkness. Melted snow and ash made mudflows.

ERUPTION ON MAY 18TH 1980

• Pumice is really lightweight frothed glass that is able to float on water.

• Pumice is used in industry as an abrasive for soft metals. It is also used for insulation in some buildings.

DEVASTATING MUDFLOWS

When Ruiz volcano in Colombia erupted in 1985, the snow melted around its summit. A mixture of water, dust, and ash fast turned to mud and buried the nearby city of Armero. More than 22,000 people were drowned in the mud.

PRODUCTS OF EXPLOSIVE VOLCANOES

ASH
Lava particles larger than dust cover the land.

LAPILLI
Lava ejected in pea-sized pieces is called lapilli.

PUMICE
Pumice is lightweight lava filled with holes.

BOMB
Bomb-shaped lava forms as it flies in the air.

PELE'S HAIR
Sometimes drops of liquid lava blow into fine spiky strands. The threads form needles of volcanic glass. They are named Pele's hair after Pele, the Hawaiian goddess of volcanoes.

NONEXPLOSIVE VOLCANOES

SOME VOLCANOES arise from fissures. Nonviscous lava flows for long distances before cooling. It builds broad plateaus or low-sided volcanoes. This kind of volcano forms at plate edges, mostly under the ocean. A hot spot volcano bursts through the middle of a plate; it is not related to plate margins.

SPREADING RIDGES
Flows of basalt lava from fissures form mountains along the edges of separating plates. These spreading ridges are usually underwater. In some places, such as Iceland, lava erupts along the crack forming rift mountains above sea level.

TYPES OF LAVA

PAHOEHOE LAVA
Lava with a wrinkled skin is called "pahoehoe." This nonviscous lava cools to form a "ropy" surface. Such flows of basalt pahoehoe lava are common in Hawaii.

AA LAVA
This is an Hawaiian word for slow-moving, viscous lava. When aa lava solidifies, it has a rough, jagged surface that is also described as blocky.

HAWAIIAN VOLCANOES
In places called hot spots, notably in Hawaii, magma rises to create lava fountains and fire curtains.

HOT SPOT VOLCANOES
The Earth's plates move slowly over hot spots in the crust. Magma rises, punching through the lithosphere to form a new island. In Hawaii, hot spots have built a chain of islands.

BASALT COLUMNS
Northern Ireland's Giant's Causeway is made of mostly hexagonal columns of basalt rock. They formed as thick lava flows cooled and vertical shrinkage cracks developed.

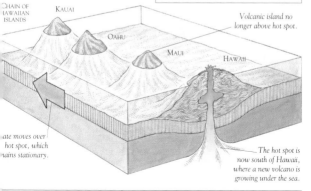

CHAIN OF HAWAIIAN ISLANDS

KAUAI

OAHU

MAUI

HAWAII

Volcanic island no longer above hot spot.

Plate moves over hot spot, which remains stationary.

The hot spot is now south of Hawaii, where a new volcano is growing under the sea.

VOLCANIC LANDSCAPES

OLD FAITHFUL
This geyser is in Yellowstone Park, Wyoming. It has shot out a column of boiling water and steam every hour for the last 100 years.

MOVEMENT IN ROCKS underground can cause changes to the landscape above. The combination of heat and water in the Earth's rocks produces various phenomena. Molten rock erupting out of the Earth brings gases, mineral deposits, and water with it. Mud pools, hot springs, and geysers form when the gases and water escape. Minerals dissolved in the hot waters precipitate to form cone-like or terraced deposits of rocks.

THE LANDSCAPE AROUND VOLCANOES

Steaming hot water

HOT SPRINGS
Magma warms water in cracks in the rock. Water returns to the surface as a hot spring.

Volcanic gases bubble through liquid mud

MUD POOLS
Steam, particles of rock, and volcanic gases bubble through pools of liquid mud.

FUMAROLES
Vents, or fumeroles, allow steam and other gases to escape from cooling rocks.

PILLOW LAVA

When lava erupts underwater it can produce these rounded shapes, which are known as "pillow lava." The seawater cools the lava rapidly, and as it solidifies a crust forms around each lump. The lava formed is typically an igneous rock called "basalt."

A NEW ISLAND

In 1963, off the southern coast of Iceland, a new volcanic island rose from the ocean floor. This island, Surtsey, formed from the buildup of lava flows. Seawater interacting with lava produced explosions and huge amounts of steam.

YSERS

at from magma
ambers causes ground
ter to boil, erupting as
s of steam and water.

TERRACES

Minerals, dissolved in heated ground water, are deposited in layers that rise around a vent.

GEYSER FACTS

• The tallest geyser is Yellowstone National Park's Steamboat Geyser in Wyoming. It reaches 195–380 ft (60–115 m).

• Strokkur Geyser in Iceland spurts every 10 to 15 minutes.

• In 1904, Waimangu Geyser, New Zealand, erupted to a height of 1,500 ft (460 m).

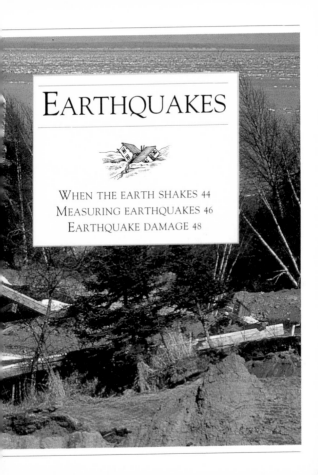

EARTHQUAKES

WHEN THE EARTH SHAKES

MORE THAN A million times a year, the Earth's crust suddenly shakes during an earthquake. Most of the world's earthquakes are fairly slight. A mild earthquake can feel like a truck passing; a severe one can destroy roads and buildings and cause the sea to rise in huge waves. Earthquakes often happen near volcanoes and young mountain ranges: at the edges of the Earth's plates.

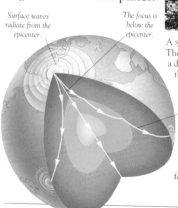

Surface waves radiate from the epicenter.

The focus is below the epicenter.

Shock waves go through the Earth and up to the surface.

A SEVERE EARTHQUAKE
The city of San Francisco was shaken a devastating earthquake in 1906. On the chimney stacks were left standi

CENTER OF AN EARTHQUA
The earthquake is strongest
the focus. At the epicenter,
point on the surface above
focus, the crust shakes and sends
shock waves. Internal waves be
as they travel through the Ear

EARTHQUAKE FAULT ZONES
Earthquakes occur at cracks in the lithosphere called "faults." Deep earthquakes take place where one plate is sliding under another.

Many earthquakes occur on the northeast coast of Asia. This is at the boundary of two of the Earth's plates.

Stress builds up in rocks along the fault line.

BEFORE AN EARTHQUAKE

AFTER AN EARTHQUAKE

The plates slip into a new position.

SLIDING PLATES
Earthquakes occur at spreading ridges, subduction zones, and transform faults, where two plates slide past each other. Stress builds up in rock and causes a sudden movement as the rock jolts into a new position. Foreshocks may precede an earthquake, and aftershocks follow it.

EARTHQUAKE FACTS

• Before some earthquakes it is reported that dogs howl, pandas moan, and well water bubbles.

• A strong earthquake can cause the ground to roll like waves at sea.

• The 1755 earthquake in Lisbon, Portugal, lasted 10 minutes. It was felt as far away as North Africa.

• About 90 percent of earthquakes occur in the Ring of Fire around the Pacific Ocean.

MEASURING EARTHQUAKES

SCIENTISTS WHO STUDY earthquakes are known as seismologists (*seismos* is the Greek word for "earthquakes. Seismologists monitor the vibrations, or shock waves, that pass through the Earth using an instrument called a "seismometer." Predicting earthquakes is very difficult. Scientists look for warnings such as bulges or small cracks on the surface of the ground.

EARTHQUAKE DESTRUCTION
In 1994, in the city of Los Angeles, an earthquake caused devastation. Roads and buildings collapsed, water mains and gas pipes burst, and fires began in the city. Many buildings in Los Angeles were built to be earthquake-proof and so did not suffer very much damage. The earthquake measured 5.7 on the Richter scale.

MERCALLI SCALE
Giuseppe Mercalli (1850–1914) devised a method of grading earthquakes based on the observation of their effects. Using this scale enables the amount of shaking, or intensity, of different earthquakes to be easily compared. On Mercalli's scale earthquakes are graded from 1 to 12.

1 • detected by instruments
2 • felt by people resting
3 • hanging lamps sway
4 • felt by people indoors
  • plates, windows rattle
  • parked cars rock

5 • buildings tremble
  • felt by most people
  • liquids spill
6 • movement felt by a
  • pictures fall off wall
  • windows break

SEISMOMETER

This device records how much the Earth shakes during an earthquake. A weight keeps the pen still while the machine holding it moves with the Earth.

A pen records the movement on a rotating drum.

...se moves with the horizontal motion of the Earth.

The recording from a seismometer is called a "seismogram." It shows an amplified wave form, resulting from the motion of the Earth's surface.

RICHTER SCALE

The amount of energy released by an earthquake can be measured on the Richter scale. An increase of 1.0 on the scale represents a tenfold increase in energy.

EARTHQUAKE	DATE	RICHTER SCALE
North Peru	1970	7.7
Mexico City	1985	7.8
Erzincan	1939	7.9
Tangshan	1976	8.0
Tokyo	1923	8.3
Kansu	1920	8.6

bricks and tiles fall
chimneys crack
difficult to stand
steering cars difficult
tree branches snap
chimneys fall

9 • some buildings collapse
  • ground cracks
  • mud oozes from ground
10 • underground pipes burst
  • river water spills out
  • most buildings collapse

11 • bridges collapse
  • railroad tracks buckle
  • landslides occur
12 • near total destruction
  • rivers change course
  • waves seen on ground

EARTHQUAKE DAMAGE

IN GENERAL, great loss of life during an earthquake can be avoided. It is often not the Earth's shaking that kills people, but falling buildings, particularly poorly constructed ones. Landslides and tsunamis also cause a lot of damage. During an average earthquake, it is best to stay indoors in a doorway or under a sturdy table. Falling masonry is a hazard outdoors.

ESTIMATED LIVES LOST AS A RESULT OF RECENT EARTHQUAKES

PLACE	YEAR	ESTIMATED DEATHS
Tangshan, China	1976	695,000
Kansu, China	1920	100,000
Tokyo, Japan	1923	99,000
Messina, Italy	1908	80,000
Armenia	1988	55,000
Northwest Iran	1990	40,000
Erzincan, Turkey	1939	30,000

FIRE HAZARD
Fire poses a great danger following an earthquake. Gas leaks and oil spills can lead to large fires like th in San Francisco in 1989.

JAPANESE PRINT SHOWING A GREAT TSUNAMI WITH MOUNT FUJI IN THE BACKGROUND.

TSUNAMIS

An earthquake on the continental shelf can start a wave at sea. Such waves have low height in deep water. As the wave nears shore, its front slows and water behind builds up to form a huge tsunami.

TSUNAMI FACTS

• The highest tsunami wave was 279 ft (85 m) high. It struck Ishigaki Island, Japan in 1971.

• In the open ocean, a tsunami can travel at speeds of 550 miles (890 km) per hour.

EARTHQUAKE-PROOF BUILDINGS

A great deal of damage is caused by buildings collapsing during earthquakes. In earthquake-prone San Francisco and Japan, there are safety guidelines that all new buildings must meet. Wooden buildings are replaced with concrete. Steel and concrete are used for foundations.

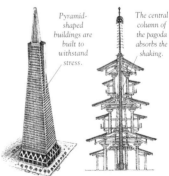

Pyramid-shaped buildings are built to withstand stress.

The central column of the pagoda absorbs the shaking.

TRANSAMERICA BUILDING, SAN FRANCISCO

ANCIENT BUDDHIST PAGODA, JAPAN

[LA]NDSLIDES

[Lo]ose rock and debris may be [dis]lodged by an earthquake [and] cause landslides as in [Ala]ska in 1964. Avalanches [ ] may be triggered by the [gro]und shaking. Mudflows, or [ ]ars, can result from rain or [ ] snow mixing with loosened soil.

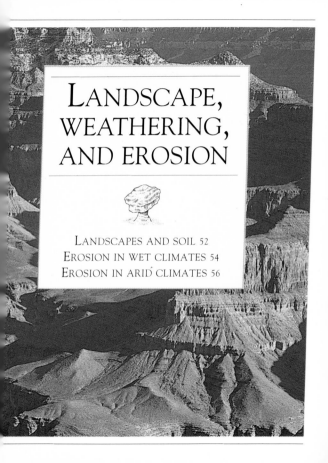

LANDSCAPE, WEATHERING, AND EROSION

LANDSCAPES AND SOIL

WEATHERING PROCESSES are primarily responsible for soil development. These processes take thousands of years. Climate, vegetation, and rock type determine what type of soil forms. Soil contains organic matter from decaying plants and animals (humus) as well as sand, silt and clay. It covers the landscape and provides a medium for plants to grow in.

PEAT LANDSCAPE
This landscape is green and low-lying. Spongy peat soil is rich in humus from decayed bog plants. It retains water and nutrients easily.

SANDY LANDSCAPE
In arid (dry) sandy landscapes there is little vegetation. The soil contains hardly any organic material. Winds blow away small particles, leaving sand and stones.

TYPES OF SOIL
Chalky soil is thin and stony; water passes through it quickly. Water drains easily through sandy soil, washing out nutrients. Clay soil retains nutrients and moisture, but is difficult for plants to take root in. Peat soil is acidic. It holds water and minerals.

CLAY

SAND

PEAT

CHALK

SOIL FACTS

• 35.3 ft³ (1 m³) of soil may contain more than 1 billion animals.

• Some soils in India, Africa, and Australia are 2 million years old.

• It can take 500 years for 1 in (2.5 cm) of topsoil to form.

SOIL PROFILE

slice of soil down to e bedrock is called a il profile. The profile ows several layers, or rizons. The number d thickness of horizons ry with the soil type.

HORIZON 0
• humus layer
• contains live and decaying plants and soil animals

HORIZON A
• topsoil
• dark and fertile
• rich in humus

HORIZON B
• subsoil
• contains minerals washed down from topsoil
• little organic matter
• lighter colored

HORIZON C
• infertile layer
• composed of weathered parent rock

HORIZON D
• bedrock (parent rock)
• source of soil's minerals

SOIL CREEP AND EROSION

ravity and water pull il down a slope particle particle. This is called il creep. Plant roots d soil and help to event it from wearing ay, or eroding. Over- azing and felling forests th lead to soil erosion.

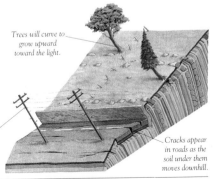

Trees will curve to grow upward toward the light.

Soil creep is indicated by leaning structures such as walls and utility poles.

Cracks appear in roads as the soil under them moves downhill.

EROSION IN WET CLIMATES

AS SOON AS ROCK is exposed on the Earth's surface, it is attacked by wind, water, or ice – a process known as "weathering." This prepares for erosion, when rock is broken down and removed. Weathering can be either physical (wearing away the rock itself) or chemical (attacking the minerals in the rock). Climate and rock type determine the kind of weathering that occurs. In wet climates, chemical weathering, mainly by rainwater, is dominant.

MOUNTAIN STREAM
Cascading over steep gradients, a swift-flowing stream wears away softer rocks. Harder rocks remain and create rocky outcrops. These become steep rapids or waterfalls.

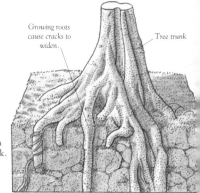

Growing roots cause cracks to widen.

Tree trunk

TREE-ROOT ACTION
As trees and other plants grow, their roots push down into small cracks in the rock. The cracks widen as the roots grow and eventually the rock breaks up.

OST SHATTERING
is type of weathering
curs when water in
cks in the rock
ezes and expands.
nts in the rock
len and the
k shatters.

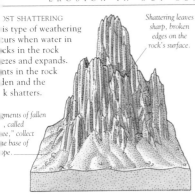

Shattering leaves sharp, broken edges on the rock's surface.

gments of fallen
, called
ee," collect
e base of
pe.

EROSION FACTS

• Acid rain can dissolve rock as deep as 98 ft (30 m) below the surface.

• Erosion is fastest in steep, rainy areas and semiarid areas with little vegetation.

• The rate of erosion for the whole of the world's land area is estimated to be 3.3 in (8.6 cm) every 1,000 years.

NTS AND GRIKES
d in rainwater seeps
o limestone joints and
solves the calcite in the
k. Ridges known as
nts" and grooves known
grikes" form in the rock.

ACID RAIN

Rainwater naturally contains a weak acid called "carbonic acid." However, the burning of fossil fuels produces gases such as sulfur dioxide. When this combines with rainwater, it produces sulfuric acid – an ingredient of "acid rain." Acid rain damages trees and lake life.

Acid rain slowly dissolves rocks such as limestone and marble.

LIMESTONE STATUES SUFFER EROSION FROM ACID RAIN

EROSION IN ARID CLIMATES

IN HOT, DRY, DESERT areas
extremes of temperature
cause rocks to fragment.
By day, rock expands in
the heat, and by night it
contracts in the cold.
It is mainly physical
weathering that occurs
in arid climates, chiefly
caused by wind. The
sand-filled wind helps
to erode rocks and build
shifting sand dunes.

Some rocks break away and fall to the ground.

Larger rock masses split into blocks.

BLOCK DISINTEGRATION
Acute temperature changes can cau
rocks to break up. Joints in the rock
grow wider with the rock's cycle of
expansion and contraction. Large
pieces split into small blocks.

ONION-SKIN LAYERING
In the heat of the desert, a rock's
surface may expand, though the
interior stays cool. At night, the
surface of the rock cools and contracts.
This daily process causes flaking on the
surface of the rock, and the outer
layers begin to peel and fall away.

SAND DUNES

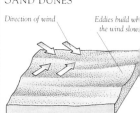

Direction of wind

*Eddies build wh
the wind slows*

LINEAR, OR SEIF, DUNE
This type of dune has long parallel
ridges. It forms where the wind blo
continually in one direction.

UGENS

nd carried by the wind
ulpts these strange forms
led "zeugens." Sand wears
way soft rock leaving
hind areas of harder rock,
rn into jagged shapes.

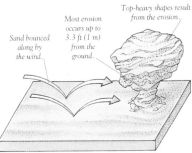

Sand bounced along by the wind.

Most erosion occurs up to 3.3 ft (1 m) from the ground.

Top-heavy shapes result from the erosion.

MUSHROOM ROCKS (PEDESTAL ROCKS)
The desert wind contains a great deal of sand,
which scours away the surface of rocks.
Mushroom-shaped rocks are a result of this action.
Rocks are worn away most at their base by the
sand, leaving behind a landscape of rock pedestals.

CROSS SECTION OF
A BARCHAN DUNE

A strong wind blows across the top of the dune.

nd slips down
e face of the
ne.

Sand builds up in the center of the dune.

Weak wind at the base of the dune

ARCHAN DUNE
sand dune with a cresent-shaped front and a
ng, sloping rear is called a "barchan dune." This
the most common dune shape for sandy deserts.

SAND DUNE FACTS

• Sand is composed
mostly of the hard
mineral quartz.

• Linear, or seif,
dunes can reach
700 ft (215 m) high.

• Not all dunes are
made of sand – dunes
can form from salt
crystals, gypsum, or
shell fragments.

• Black sand dunes
form in volcanic areas.

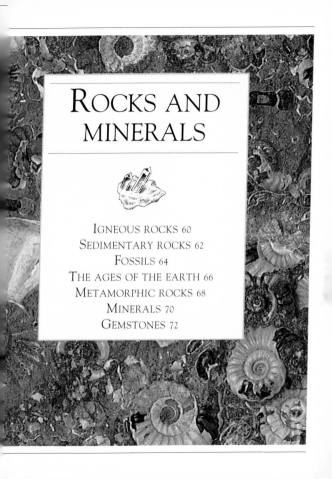

ROCKS AND MINERALS

IGNEOUS ROCKS

MAGMA THAT COOLS solidifies into igneous rocks.
The rock material of the lower lithosphere and
mantle is semimolten. Sudden
release of confining pressure
allows this material to change
to liquid magma. Magma that
cools and solidifies under
the Earth's surface forms
intrusive igneous rock.
If it erupts as lava from a
volcano and cools on the
Earth's surface it forms
extrusive igneous rock.

INTRUSIVE IGNEOUS ROCK
Sugar Loaf Mountain, Brazil,
formed from magma that solidified
under-ground. Eventually, the
surrounding rock eroded, leaving
this dome shape.

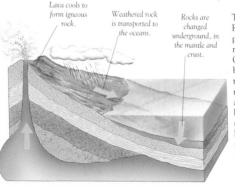

Lava cools to form igneous rock.

Weathered rock is transported to the oceans.

Rocks are changed underground, in the mantle and crust.

THE ROCK CYCLE
Rocks constantly
pass through a
recycling process.
Crustal movement
bring igneous rock
to the surface. The
rocks weather away
and the particles
build sedimentary
rocks. Pressure and
heat underground
may change, or
metamorphose,
rocks before
they reemerge.

SYDNEY HARBOR BRIDGE
The supporting pylons of this famous bridge in Sydney, Australia are built from granite. The span of the bridge is 1,650 ft (503 m) and the arch is made of steel. Granite is often used as a building material because of its strength and availability.

IGNEOUS ROCK FACTS
• Basalt makes up most of the ocean floor.
• Obsidian was used in early jewelry and tools.
• Most continental igneous rocks are quartz, feldspar, and mica.
• Earth's first rocks were igneous rocks.

TYPES OF IGNEOUS ROCK

Shell-like, curved fracture

OBSIDIAN
This natural glass forms from rapid cooling of granitic lava.

Granite has coarse grains

GABBRO
This intrusive, coarse-grained rock forms from slow-cooled lava.

BASALT
Nonviscous lava that flows great distances forms fine-grained basalt.

PINK GRANITE
Granite is a common intrusive rock. Crystals of pink feldspar, black mica, and gray quartz minerals are visible.

SEDIMENTARY ROCKS

ROCK IS GRADUALLY weakened by
the weather. Particles of rock are
then carried off by rain or wind.
These particles build up into layers
of sediment. Evaporation of ground
water may leave behind minerals,
such as silica, calcium carbonate,
and iron oxides, that cement the
sediment grains (a process
known as "lithification").
Studying sedimentary rock
layers can reveal ancient
environments.

STRATA
Over millions of years, layers
of sediment are cemented in
bands of rock called "strata."
Strata in the Grand Canyon
Arizona preserve a record of
the region's history.

FLINT TOOLS
Prehistoric people fashioned
tools from a sedimentary
rock called "flint." Flint was
chipped into shape using a
stone. It is a common rock
that flakes easily, leaving a
sharp edge. Prehistoric
tools such as hand axes
and adzes (for shaping
wood) have been found.

FLINT
ADZE

CHALK CLIFFS
These cliffs in Sussex, England,
are a type of limestone. They ar
calcium carbonate (chalk) and
contain fossils of microorganism

EGYPTIAN PYRAMIDS AT GIZA
Elaborate tombs (begun c. 2686) for the Egyptian
Pharaohs were constructed at Giza, Egypt. They were
built from nummulitic limestone, which contains
many large marine fossils called *Nummulites*.

SEDIMENTARY FACTS

- Chalk consists of tiny shells, visible only under a microscope.

- Mudstone forms from compressed mud grains, and sandstone from compressed sand grains.

- Oil is usually found in permeable and porous sandstones.

TYPES OF SEDIMENTARY ROCK

BRECCIA
Angular fragments of
rock are cemented
together to form
a breccia.

CHALK
Skeletons of tiny sea
animals form this type
of limestone. Chalk is
fine grained and soft.

RED SANDSTONE
Cemented sand grains
coated with iron
oxide make up this
sedimentary rock.

SHELLY LIMESTONE
This rock contains a
great many fossils cemented
together with calcite.
Limestone usually forms in
a shallow sea, though it can
come from a freshwater
environment. It is possible
to find the source of a
specimen by studying the
fossils it contains.

FOSSILS

PLANTS AND ANIMALS that lived millions of
years ago are preserved in rocks as fossils.
A fossil is the remains of an organism, a
cast of an animal or plant made from
minerals, or even burrows or tracks
left by animals and preserved in
rock. Sedimentary rocks such
as limestone or chalk hold
fossils. Paleontologists are
scientists who study fossils.

PLANT FOSSIL
Seed ferns like this one were widespread in the
hot swamps of the late Carboniferous period.
These primitive land plants, with some
adaptations, still exist today.

THE FOSSILIZATION PROCESS

1 When an animal or
plant dies underwater, it
falls to the seabed. The
soft parts of its body decay
or are eaten by animals.

2 The organism is buried
in layers of sediment.
Hard parts of the animal,
such as the shell, bones, or
teeth, are preserved.

3 Minerals in the se
react with the an
shell to harden it
animals decay, leavin
space where a cast fo

SEED FERN
(ALETHOPTERIS)

INSECT FOSSIL
Early dragonflies, preserved in limestone, have been found in Europe and Australasia. This one dates from the Jurassic period.

DRAGONFLY
(PETALURA)

FISH FOSSIL
Fish are the most primitive vertebrates (animals with backbones). This fish first appeared 24.5 to 30 million years ago, long after the dinosaurs had died out.

FISH FROM THE OLIGOCENE PERIOD

Further sediments cover the fossil. Uplift of the lithosphere or ~~sion~~ may eventually ~~ose~~ the fossil.

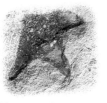

TRACE FOSSILS
Fossilized droppings or tracks are called "trace fossils." This dinosaur footprint was left in mud 135 million years ago.

FOSSIL FACTS

• Dated at about 230 million years old, the earliest dinosaur bones were found in 1999 in Madagascar.

• The largest fossil footprint was left by a hadrosaurid. It is 53.5 in (1.36 m) long.

• Fossils of cells are the first evidence of life, 3.2 billion years ago.

THE AGES OF THE EARTH

THE LARGEST DIVISIONS of Earth's history are eras, periods, and epochs. The timescale is marked by the appearance of new life-forms. Life on Earth is never static – it constantly changes and evolves. Creatures become extinct and others appear. Some types of creatures may be short-lived and others survive unchanged for millions of years. Fossils can build up a picture of life in the past

JELLYFISH FOSSIL

PRECAMBRIAN FOSSIL
This fossil is about 570 million years old. It is a kind of primitive jellyfish that lived in Australia.

MORE FOSSIL FACTS

• Our species, *Homo sapiens*, appeared at least 100,000 years ago.

• A million Ice Age fossils were found preserved in the tar pits of La Brea, California.

CARBONIFEROUS SWAMP
Extensive swamps covered Earth in the Mississippi and Pennsylvanian periods (290–363 million years ago). It was during this time that forests, containing seed plants and ferns, flourished. Some of these were preserved and now form coal deposits. The first reptiles and giant dragonflies lived in these swamps

DILOPHOSAURUS
(TWO-RIDGED LIZARD)

Distinguishing tall, double crest on the skull

THE DINOSAUR AGE
During the Triassic period, the first land-dwelling dinosaurs appeared. The ...e of the dinosaurs lasted through ...Jurassic and Cretaceous periods.

HOMO
HABILIS SKUL

...RLY HUMANS
...mo habilis (handy man) is an ...rly human, dating from the ...aternary period. The name of ...s ancestor comes from the fossil ...idence that the early human ...s skilled in using crude tools.

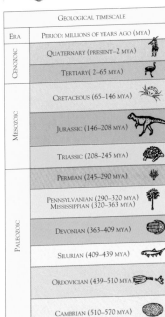

GEOLOGICAL TIMESCALE		
ERA	PERIOD: MILLIONS OF YEARS AGO (MYA)	
CENOZOIC	QUATERNARY (PRESENT–2 MYA)	
	TERTIARY (2–65 MYA)	
MESOZOIC	CRETACEOUS (65–146 MYA)	
	JURASSIC (146–208 MYA)	
	TRIASSIC (208–245 MYA)	
PALEOZOIC	PERMIAN (245–290 MYA)	
	PENNSYLVANIAN (290–320 MYA) MISSISSIPPIAN (320–363 MYA)	
	DEVONIAN (363–409 MYA)	
	SILURIAN (409–439 MYA)	
	ORDOVICIAN (439–510 MYA)	
	CAMBRIAN (510–570 MYA)	
	PRECAMBRIAN (570–4,600 MYA)	

METAMORPHIC ROCKS

SLATE MOUNTAINS
Fine-grained slate forms from sedimentary rocks. Rocks such as shale or mudstone are compressed during mountain building and changed into slate. Slate's aligned crystals let it split, or cleave, easily into flat sheets.

SEDIMENTARY, metamorphic, or igneous rocks are remade into new metamorphic rocks. The rock doesn't melt, but it is changed underground by pressure and heat. During mountain building, in particular, intense pressure over millions of years alters the texture and nature of rocks. Igneous rocks such as granite change into gneiss and sedimentary rocks like limestone into marble.

Carved white marble

MARBLE SCULPTURE
Michelangelo's statue of David is carved in marble. Marble comes in many varieties. It is a relatively soft rock that is often sculpted.

METAMORPHIC FACTS

• The oldest rock on Earth is a metamorphic rock. It is Amitsoc gneiss from Amitsoc Bay, Greenland.

• Rubies are found in metamorphic limestone in the Himalayas. They formed during mountain building.

GIONAL METAMORPHISM
treme pressure and heat created
ring mountain building lead to
gional metamorphism.
etamorphism
 this scale
n cover
ast
ea.

Migmatite showing swirls of folded rock

Intrusive igneous rock
exposed by weathering.

Aureole (area where
metamorphism has
taken place)

CONTACT METAMORPHISM
Rocks near to a lava flow or to an intrusion
of igneous rock can be altered by contact
metamorphism. This metamorphism affects a
small area and is generated by heat alone.

TYPES OF METAMORPHIC ROCK

SLATE
Mica crystals lie in the
ame direction in slate,
naking it easy to split.

SCHIST
Formed in moderate
pressure and temperature
conditions, schist often
shows small, wavy folds.

MARBLE
When limestone is
ubjected to intense
eat it becomes marble.

GNEISS
Igneous and sedimentary
rocks can become gneiss. It
forms at high temperatures.

CALCITE

Perfect cleavage plane through the crystal.

MINERALS

ROCKS ARE MADE from non-living, natural substances called "minerals," which may be alone or in combination. Marble is pure calcite, for example, but granite is a mixture of quartz, feldspars, and mica. Most minerals are formed from silicates (compounds of oxygen and silicon). Minerals with regular arrangements of atoms may form large regular crystals. To identify a mineral, properties such as crystal structure, color and hardness are tested.

CLEAVAGE AND FRACTURE
Diamond and calcite cleave when they break. Cleavage is a smooth break between layers of atoms in a crystal. A fracture is an uneven break, not related to the internal atomic structure. Most minerals fracture and cleave.

MOHS'S SCALE
A German mineralogist named Friedrich Mohs devised a scale to compare the hardness of different minerals. A mineral is able to scratch any others below it on the scale and can be scratched by any mineral above it.

1	2	3	4
TALC	GYPSUM	CALCITE	FLUORITE

PLAGIOCLASE FELDSPAR

QUARTZ OR ROCK CRYSTAL

FELDSPAR
This type of rock-forming mineral is in both basalt and granite.

QUARTZ
A common mineral, quartz comes in many different colors. Amethyst and citrine are varieties of quartz.

COLOR STREAKS
Scratching a mineral on an unglazed tile produces a colored streak. The color of the powder left behind is known as the mineral's "streak."

A light aluminum-rich mica

MUSCOVITE

ORPIMENT - GOLDEN HEMATITE - RED/BROWN

MICA
Found in metamorphic rocks such as schists and slate, flaky mica is also in igneous rocks like granite.

5	6	7	8	9	10
ATITE	ORTHOCLASE FELDSPAR	QUARTZ	TOPAZ	CORUNDUM	DIAMOND

GEMSTONES

ONLY ABOUT 50 OF Earth's
3,000 minerals are valued as
gemstones. Minerals such as
diamonds, sapphires, emeralds,
and rubies are commonly used
as gems. They are chosen for
their rarity, durability, color,
and optical qualities. Gems may
be found embedded in rocks
or washed into the gravel of a
river. Organic gemstones have
a plant or animal origin. They
include pearl, amber, and coral.

Red spinels
were often
mistaken for
rubies.

The crown
contains more
than 3,000
stones.

CROWN JEWELS
The British Imperial State
Crown contains the Black
Prince's ruby (in fact, a
170-carat spinel) and the
famous Cullinan II diamond.

EMERALD
Green beryl crystals
called "emeralds"
contain chromium to
make them green.
Most emeralds are
mined in Colombia.
They have a hardness
of 7.5 on Mohs's scale.

Emerald is found
in granites and
pegmatites.

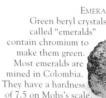

KIMBERLITE
Diamonds used
to be found mainly in
river gravels in India.
In 1870, diamonds were
discovered in volcanic
rock, called kimberlite,
in South Africa.

BRILLIANT
Skilled gem cutters, known
as "lapidaries," cut a rough
crystal into a sparkling stone.
A diamond has 58 facets, or
faces, cut and polished on its
surface to make it a brilliant.

SYNTHETIC GEMS

me gems can be
roduced almost
actly in a laboratory.
ssolved minerals and
oring agents
stallize under strictly
ntrolled conditions
produce perfect
stals. Synthetic
stals are used in
dicine and the
ctronics industry.

NATURAL
RUBY

SYNTHETIC RUBY

IMITATION TURQUOISE

REAL TURQUOISE

MITATION GEMS
lass or plastic may be
sed to imitate gems.
he optical properties
f such imitations are
ifferent from those
f the genuine gem.

PEARL

Shellfish, such as
mussels and
oysters, grow
pearls in their
shells. When a
grain of sand
lodges
in its shell, the
animal covers
it with nacre, a
substance to
stop irritation.
This creates a pearl.

AMBER

Fossilized resin from
coniferous trees is called
"amber." The trees that
yielded this amber
existed more than 300
million years ago and
are extinct. Amber
may contain insects
trapped in the tree sap.

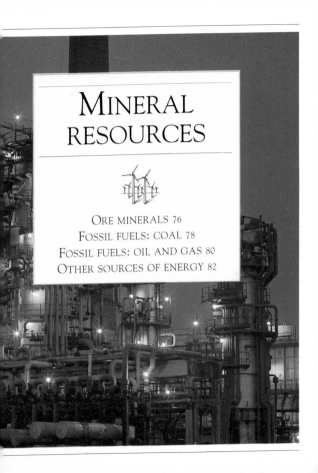

MINERAL RESOURCES

ORE MINERALS

A ROCK THAT yields metal in sufficient amounts is a metallic ore. Gold and copper can be found as pure metals, that is, uncombined with any other elements. Most other metals, such as iron and tin, are extracted from ores. Mined or quarried rock is crushed. The ore is separated and purified.

IRON ORE (HEMATITE)

ALUMINUM ORE (BAUXITE)

ALUMINUM FOIL

ALUMINUM
Lightweight aluminum is a good conductor of electricity and resists corrosion. It is extracted from its main ore (bauxite) by passing an electric current through molten bauxite and chemical fluxes.

GOLD FACTS

• The largest pure gold nugget weighed 142.5 (70.9 kg). It was found in Victoria, Australia.

• 60 percent of the world's gold is mined in South Africa.

• Gold never loses its luster or shine.

• It is said that all the gold ever mined would fit into an average four bedroom house.

MERCURY
THERMOMETER

MERCURY ORE
(CINNABAR)

N

...matite is an important
...n ore. Iron can be cast,
...ged, and alloyed with
...er metals. Steel, used in
... building and industry,
...roduced using iron.

MERCURY
The primary mercury ore is called
"cinnabar." It is found near volcanic
vents and hot springs, mostly in
China, Spain, and Italy. Mercury is
liquid at room temperature.

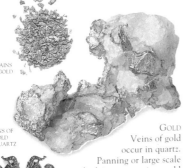

...AINS
...OLD

...NS OF
...OLD
...UARTZ

GOLD GRIFFIN
BRACELET

MINING
Blasting and boring
rock in underground
mines allows recovery
of ores such as gold or
tin. Dredging gravel
or quarrying rock also
retrieves ores.

GOLD
Veins of gold
occur in quartz.
Panning or large scale
dredging can retrieve gold
grains from sand or river
gravel deposits. About 1,500
tons (tonnes) of gold are
produced each year.

FOSSIL FUELS: COAL

PLANTS THAT GREW millions of years ago slowly changed to form coal. Vegetation in swamp areas, buried under layers of sediment, forms a substance called "peat." Peat, in turn, is pressed into a soft coal called "lignite." Soft, bituminous coal forms under further pressure. Anthracite is the hardest and most compressed coal. When coal burns, the energy of the ancient plants is released. Coal is used to fuel power stations that produce electricity. Coal supplies, like oil, are finite.

PEAT

LIGNITE

BITUMINOUS COAL

ANTHRACITE

FROM PEAT TO COAL
Heat and pressure change crumbly brown peat into hard, black, anthracite co

---

COAL FORMATION

Vegetation

PEAT LAYER
In swamps, when plants decay they form a compact layer called peat. This material is 60 percent carbon and can be burned as a fuel.

Layers of sediment

Temperature and pressure increases.

COAL LAYER
Buried beneath sediment layers, compacted peat forms coal. Lignite is the softest coal and anthracite the hardest coal.

INSIDE A COAL MINE
To reach a seam, or layer, of coal underground, rock must be blasted and bored away. Shafts go down from the surface to tunnels at different levels. Rock pillars and walls support the roof.

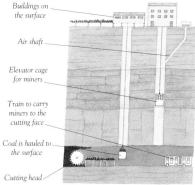

Buildings on the surface

Air shaft

Elevator cage for miners

Train to carry miners to the cutting face

Coal is hauled to the surface

Cutting head

...AL MINING
...ople have mined coal ...ce about 500 B.C. ...day's miners use drills ...d computer-controlled ...chines. Special cutting ...chines dig out the coal ...the coal face. Deep coal ...nes deliver 2,000 tons ...nnes) of coal a day.

...P OF COAL DEPOSITS
...ampy forests covered parts ...urope, Asia, and North ...erica, which were ...-lying during the ...rboniferous ...iod (286 – ...) million ...rs ago). ...ese tropical ...st areas ...vide most ...he coal ...osits that are ...ed today.

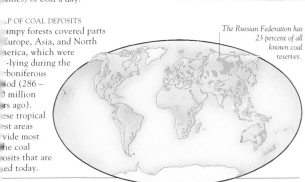

The Russian Federation has 23 percent of all known coal reserves.

FOSSIL FUELS: OIL AND GAS

MOST SCIENTISTS believe oil and gas are derived from the remains of ancient, single-cell marine animals. The organic remains were decomposed over millions of years to form oil and gas. The source rocks were compressed and heated to form liquid and gas hydrocarbons. Then they migrated to porous reservoir rocks that form oil and gas traps.

OIL RIG
An oil production platform floats, but is tethered to the seabed. Oil is pumped up lon pipelines to the oil platform.

OIL AND GAS FORMATION

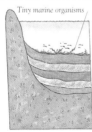

Tiny marine organisms

New layers of sediment

Oil and gas rigs *Fuels colle under sol caproc*

1 Decaying plants and animals sink to the seafloor. They lie buried by accumulating layers of sediment.

2 Heat and pressure increase as the sediments sink deeper. The organic remains become oil and gas.

3 Molecules of gas and oil rise through permeable rock and are held in porous rock.

PRODUCTS MADE FROM OIL
Crude oil is separated into products such as paraffin, gasoline, and propane gas in a refinery. Further processing (cracking) produces chemicals used to manufacture paints, textiles, plastics, and many other products.

SWEATER MADE FROM
SYNTHETIC FIBERS

INFLATABLE TOY MADE
FROM THIN PLASTIC

PAINT

PLASTIC TOY

OIL USED IN MACHINERY AND VEHICLES

AP OF OIL AND GAS DEPOSITS
l has been found in places such the Middle East and e Arctic. North d Central merica also ve large and gas lds.

There are large oil deposits in the North Sea.

st gas fields in the US, ecially Alaska, l in the Russian deration, usually se to oil deposits.

OTHER SOURCES OF ENERGY

MOST OF THE energy the world uses
for cooking, heating, or industry is
produced by burning fossil fuels.
These fuels cause pollution and will
eventually run out. The Sun, wind,
or water can be used to create
pollution-free energy. This energy
is renewable for as long as the Sun
shines, the wind blows, and the tides
rise and fall. At present most of the
electrical energy we use at home is
generated by fossil and nuclear fuels.

SOLAR ENERGY
The Sun's light energy i
concentrated by huge
mirrors. The energy is us
to generate electricity.

TIDAL POWER
Inexpensive power can be generated
in estuaries that have a large height
difference between low and high tide,
such as the Bay of Fundy in the US and
Canada. Power can be generated both as
the tide rises and as it falls.

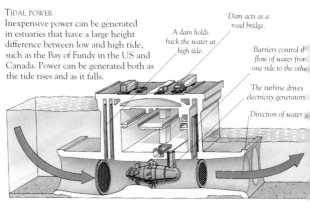

A dam holds
back the water at
high tide.

Dam acts as a
road bridge.

Barriers control th
flow of water from
one side to the othe

The turbine drives
electricity generators

Direction of water

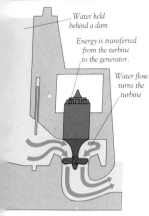

Water held behind a dam

Energy is transferred from the turbine to the generator.

Water flow turns the turbine

NUCLEAR ENERGY

Elements such as plutonium and uranium are used in nuclear power stations to generate energy. An atom of uranium can be split using a particle called a "neutron." This produces heat and other neutrons. In turn, these neutrons split more atoms, generating further energy.

Neutron hits uranium atom

The nucleus of the uranium atom splits.

More neutrons are made

WATER POWER

A hydroelectric power station uses water power to produce electricity. The energy created by falling water turns a turbine that turns an electric generator.

ENERGY FACTS

• The first tidal power station opened in La Rance, France, in 1966.

• Nuclear power first produced electricity in the US in 1951.

• Hydroelectric power stations generate 5 percent of all electricity.

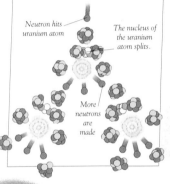

WIND POWER

California has wind farms that contain thousands of windmills. Persistent winds spin the propellers, which drive electric generators. Each windmill can produce up to 300 kilowatts of power.

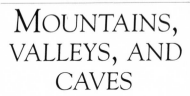

MOUNTAINS, VALLEYS, AND CAVES

THE WORLD'S MOUNTAINS

SOME MOUNTAIN ridges on land result from the collision of continental masses riding on tectonic plates. The Alps and Himalayas formed in this way. These lofty peaks continue to form as the Indian plate pushes the Eurasian plate. As the rocky plates fracture and crumple (or fault and fold) a mountain range takes shape. Our planet has had several mountain-building episodes during its history. Some mountains are rising faster than they are being weathered awa

ANCIENT MOUNTAINS
The Scottish Highlands have been eroded into low, rounded hills. These ancient mountains formed more than 250 million years ago.

YOUNG MOUNTAINS
Mountains such as the Himalayas continue to rise. The mountains are about 50 million years old and have jagged peaks.

TYPES OF MOUNTAIN

FAULT-BLOCK MOUNTAIN
When Earth's plates push into one another, faults or cracks in the crust appear. Huge blocks of rock are forced upward.

FOLD MOUNTAIN
At the meeting of two continents, the crust buckles and bends. The rocky crust is forced up into a mountain range.

MOUNTAINS AND MOUNTAIN RANGES
The world's longest mountain ranges
usually follow the edges of the
Earth's plates.

Mount El'brus,
Russia:18,510 ft
(5,642 m) high

Himalaya-Karakoram
Hindu Kush: 2,400
miles (3,800 km) long

Rocky Mountains:
3,000 miles
(4,800 km) long

Andes: 4,500 miles
(7,200 km) long

Mt. Kilimanjaro,
Tanzania: 19,340 ft
(5,895 m) high

Trans-Antarctic:
2,200 miles
3,500 km) long

Great Dividing
Range:2,240 miles
(3,600 km) long

VOLCANO
Lava from a deep magma
chamber may erupt to
form a volcano. A tall
cone builds up from lava,
ash, and rock ejected
from the volcano.

DOME MOUNTAIN
Rising magma forces up
rocks near the surface.
A dome-shaped
mountain results.

MOUNTAIN FACTS

• The ten highest
mountains on land are
all in the Himalayas.

• Europe's Alps are part
of a mountain belt that
stretches from the
Pyrenees in Europe to
the Himalayas in Asia.

• The Himalayas grow
at a rate of 3.3 ft (1 m)
every 1,000 years.

• The Alps are the
youngest of the world's
great mountain ranges.

MOUNTAIN FEATURES

CONDITIONS ON MOUNTAINS can be harsh. As altitude increases temperature drops, air becomes thinner, and winds blow harder. Animal and plant life has adapted to survive in this environment. Mountains can be divided into several separate zones. The zones are similar whether the mountain lies in a tropical or temperate area and whether it is an isolated volcanic peak or part of a mountain range.

MOUNT KILIMANJARO
Africa's tallest mountain is Mount Kilimanjaro in Tanzania. It is a solitary peak, not part of a range. In fact, it is a dormant volcanic cone. Despite lying near the equator, Kilimanjaro is permanently snowcapped.

WORLD'S HIGHEST MOUNTAINS PER CONTINENT

MOUNTAIN	CONTINENT	HEIGHT IN FEET	HEIGHT IN METERS
Mt. Everest, Nepal	Asia	29,028	8,848
Mt. Aconcagua, Argentina	South America	22,834	6,960
Mt. McKinley, Alaska	North America	20,320	6,194
Mt. Kilimanjaro, Tanzania	Africa	19,340	5,895
Mt. El'brus, Russia	Europe	18,510	5,642
Vinson Massif	Antarctica	16,863	5,140
Mt. Wilhelm, Papua New Guinea	Australasia	16,024	4,884

THE ANDES
The world's longest range mountains on land is the Andes in South America. The chain stretches for 4,500 miles (7,200 km).

UNDERSEA MOUNTAIN

Measured from the ocean floor, Mauna Kea, Hawaii, is taller than Mount Everest. Rising 13,796 ft (4,205 m) above sea level, its base lies in a trough under the sea.

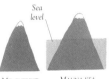

Sea level

MT. EVEREST
29,028 FT
(8,848 M)

MAUNA KEA
33,480 FT
(10,205 M)

MORE MOUNTAIN FACTS

• On a mountain, the temperature drops 1.1°F (0.7°C) for every 330 ft (100 m) climbed.

• In warm Equatorial regions trees can grow at heights of 13,124 ft (4,000 m).

MOUNTAIN VEGETATION

As the altitude increases, the temperature falls. This effect produces distinct vegetation and climate zones. The plant and animal life of each zone varies. These are the zones of the European Alps.

Rocks permanently covered with snow support no plant or animal life.

Permanent snowline

Loose rock, or scree, fractured by the weathering process

Alpine plants and flowers in pastureland have adapted to survive in the cold air.

Coniferous forest

Deciduous forests grow at the base of the mountain.

VALLEYS

FORCES OF EROSION, especially water, control the shape of the landscape. Steep-sided valleys can be cut by fast-flowing mountain streams. Larger rivers wear a path through the land, shaping wide, flat valleys as they near the sea. Frozen water in glaciers also erodes rock, forming deep, icy gullies. Valleys sometimes form as a result of crustal movements that pull rocks apart at steep faults in the Earth's surface rocks.

GORGE
A ravine with steep sides is called a gorge. A canyon is similar to a gorge, but it is usually found in desert areas.

The lithosphere drops between the plate edges.

RIFT VALLEY
Faults occur in the Earth's crust where two plates are moving apart. A long, straight valley, such as the African Rift Valley, forms between the faults.

Rivers shed their sediments on the flat floodplain.

A fan-shaped delta forms at the river mouth.

FJORD
Steep-sided estuaries such as those in Norway and New Zealand, are caused by glaciers deepening river valleys. As the ice melts and the sea level rises, the fjords flood.

VALLEY FACTS
• Africa's Rift Valley stretches for 2,500 miles (4,000 km).

• The longest fjord, in Nordvest, Greenland, is 194 miles (313 km) long.

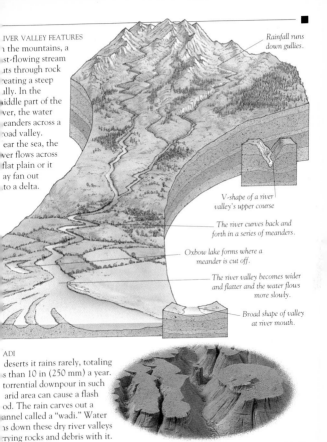

RIVER VALLEY FEATURES
In the mountains, a fast-flowing stream cuts through rock creating a steep gully. In the middle part of the river, the water meanders across a broad valley. Near the sea, the river flows across a flat plain or it may fan out into a delta.

Rainfall runs down gullies.

V-shape of a river valley's upper course

The river curves back and forth in a series of meanders.

Oxbow lake forms where a meander is cut off.

The river valley becomes wider and flatter and the water flows more slowly.

Broad shape of valley at river mouth.

WADI
In deserts it rains rarely, totaling less than 10 in (250 mm) a year. A torrential downpour in such an arid area can cause a flash flood. The rain carves out a channel called a "wadi." Water runs down these dry river valleys carrying rocks and debris with it.

CAVES

UNDERGROUND CAVERNS and caves occur in several types of landscape. Different processes are responsible for the development of caves. The action of ice, lava, waves, and rainwater cause subterranean openings. In particular, rainwater has a spectacular effect on limestone, producing vast caverns full of unusual shapes.

ICE CAVE
Beneath a glacier there is sometimes a stream of water that has thawed, called "meltwater." The water can wear away an ice cave full of icicles in the glacier.

INSIDE A LIMESTONE CAVE
Carbonic acid in rain seeps into cracks in limestone and dissolves the rock. Under-ground tunnels and caves form as water dissolves the rock. Streams may flow down sinkholes in the rock into a cave system and emerge in another place.

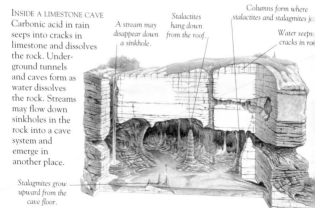

A stream may disappear down a sinkhole.

Stalactites hang down from the roof.

Columns form where stalactites and stalagmites jo

Water seeps cracks in ro

Stalagmites grow upward from the cave floor.

LAVA CAVE
Some lava cools to form a thick crust. Below the crust a tube of molten lava flows. When it empties a cave remains.

LAVA CAVE
Caves may form at the base of cliffs undercut by erosion. A cave can be worn through to form an arch. The top of this arch may eventually collapse and leave an isolated stack to be buffeted by the waves.

STALAGMITES AND STALACTITES

STALACTITE
In limestone caves, deposits of calcite left by dripping water create distinctive features, such as stalactites. These grow from the ceiling of the cave toward the floor.

COLUMNS
Mineral deposits construct stalactites and stalagmites in caves. If the two shapes meet, they form a column.

STALAGMITE
It may take several thousand years for a stalagmite to grow 1 in (2.5 cm) – drip by drip, from a cave floor to the roof.

GLACIATION

THE WORLD'S GLACIERS

A GLACIER IS a mass of moving ice that originates in mountainous regions (mountain glaciers) or large, cold regions (ice caps). Ice builds up where there is more winter snow than melts in summer. The thick snow is compressed into ice. When the ice becomes very thick it begins to flow under its weight. Mountain glaciers are ice streams that follow former river valleys as they carry rock debris downhill.

GLACIAL DEBRIS
Rocks are smoothed when they are plucked up and carried along by a glacier. This rock has scratches, or striae, too.

Ridge or arête between two glaciers

Medial moraine – debris carried in the middle of the glacier

When the ice moves a sharp incline, it cre to form crevasses

THE WORLD'S LONGEST GLACIERS

GLACIERS	LENGTH IN MILES	LENGTH IN KM
Lambert-Fisher Ice Passage, Antarctica	320	515
Novaya Zemlya, Russia	260	418
Arctic Institute Ice Passage, Antarctica	225	362
Nimrod-Lennox-King, Antarctica	180	289
Denman Glacier, Antarctica	150	241
Beardmore Glacier, Antarctica	140	225
Recovery Glacier, Antarctica	124	200

BEFORE GLACIATION
[Th]e mountain valley
[car]ved out by a river is
[us]ually steep and shaped
[lik]e the letter V.

AFTER GLACIATION
A mountain glacier flows
along the path of a river.
The V-shape is eroded by
the glacier into a U-shape.

CROSS-SECTION
OF A GLACIER

*Cirque or corrie – hollow
where glacier begins*

Compact snow called firn

FEATURES OF A GLACIER
A glacier begins high in the mountains in
hollows called "cirques." New snow builds up
and becomes compacted, forming denser ice
called "firn." As the glacier moves downhill,
it collects soil and rock from the floor and
sides of the valley and carries it along. The
rock debris carried by the glacier erodes the
valley. The debris accumulates as moraine at
the front of the melting glacier.

*The snout or front
of the glacier*

*Meltwater
flows from the
snout*

*Pile of rocks
and boulders
called "terminal
moraine"*

ICE CAPS AND ICE AGES

ANTARCTICA AND GREENLAND are blanketed in ice sheets up to 11,500 ft (3,500 m) thick. Many winters of snowfall accumulate to produce an ice cap, which eventually moves downhill as a broad glacial mass. In Earth's history, periods of extreme cold, called ice ages, brought glacial conditions as far south as Europe and North America. Our mild climate may only be an interval between ice ages.

ICE CAP
Vast ice sheets covering Antarctica and Greenland are known as "ice caps."

FORMATION OF AN ICE CAP
Layers of snow build up during the winter months and become icy firn. Over many years, the result is a thick ice cap. Gravity pulls the ice down to the edges of the land.

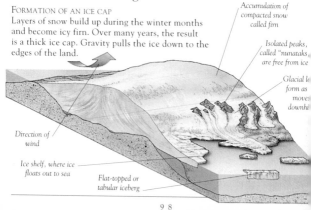

Accumulation of compacted snow called firn

Isolated peaks, called "nunataks" are free from ice

Glacial le form as move downhi

Direction of wind

Ice shelf, where ice floats out to sea

Flat-topped or tabular iceberg

RAPH OF THE EARTH'S TEMPERATURE
he low points on the graph show the
me when the average earth
mperature was cold enough to allow
ajor glacial advances.

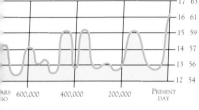

CLIMATE	
°C	°F
17	63
16	61
15	59
14	57
13	56
12	54

ARS 600,000   400,000   200,000   PRESENT
GO   DAY

ICE FACTS

• Most of the world's
freshwater – 75 percent
of it – is stored in ice
caps and glaciers.

• About 12 percent of
the sea and 10 percent
of the land is presently
covered in ice.

• Almost 90 percent of
the world's ice lies in
the continent of
Antarctica.

E AGES

uring the last ice age, about
,000 years ago, ice sheets
vered a large part of Earth,
rticularly North America
d northern Europe. All ice
es are interspersed with
rmer periods called
terglacials." Ice advanced
d retreated with each
jor temperature change.

PLEISTOCENE EPOCH
– THE LAST ICE AGE

EXTENT OF ICE IN
THE WORLD TODAY

SCIENTISTS EXAMINE
A BABY MAMMOTH
FOUND IN THE ICE

WOOLLY MAMMOTH
In Siberia, the remains of extinct
animals called "mammoths" have
been found in ice. They froze so
quickly that their bodies were
preserved virtually intact. These
elephantlike mammals had curled
tusks and woolly coats and lived
during the last ice age.

AVALANCHES AND ICEBERGS

MOUNTAINS ARE inhospitable places. Winter snowstorms pile up layers of ice and snow. The layers may become unstable and swoop down the mountain in an avalanche, destroying anything in their path. Icebergs form when large chunks of ice break off (calve) from coastal glaciers or ice shelves. These are carried out to sea by ocean currents and are a hazard to ships.

SEA ICE
Seawater freezes when it reaches 28°F (−1.9°C). Sea ice is never more than about 16 ft (5 m) thick. It can be used as a source of freshwater because the salt is left behind in the sea.

AVALANC
Vibrations from no and minor earthquak combined wit rise in temperatu especially in spri can trigger a fal snow, called "avalanch

A heavy snowfall adds weight to the snow cover.

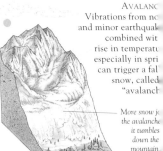

More snow jo the avalanche it tumbles down the mountain.

SNOWLINE

There is an elevation on a mountainside, called the "snowline," below which snow melts during summer. Above this elevation the snow remains throughout the year. The snowline is higher in more equatorial regions.

The snowline in the European Alps is at about 9,000 ft (2,700 m) high.

In Antarctica, the snowline is at or near sea level.

On the equator the snowline is 16,000 ft (4,900 m) high.

ICEBERGS

Glaciers and the floating edges of ice caps lose chunks of ice called "icebergs" into the sea, a process known as "calving." All icebergs are frozen freshwater, rather than frozen seawater.

ICEBERG FACTS

• Only 12 percent of an iceberg can be seen above the ocean. 88 percent is under the water.

• The tallest iceberg was sighted in 1958 off Greenland. It was 550 ft (167 m) high.

• The largest iceberg, spotted in the Pacific Ocean in 1956, had an area of 12,500 miles^2 (32,500 km^2).

OCEANS, ISLANDS, AND COASTS

THE WORLD'S OCEANS

SEEN FROM SPACE, the Earth looks blue and watery. This is because two-thirds of it is covered with water. The water is held in oceans and seas. (Seas are surrounded by land.) There are five oceans: three are in the Southern Hemisphere. Major currents circulate the oceans counter-clockwise in the Southern Hemisphere and clockwise in the Northern Hemisphere.

THE WORLD'S LARGEST OCEANS AND SEAS

OCEAN OR SEA	AREA IN MILES^2	AREA IN KM^2
Pacific Ocean	64,181,000	166,229,000
Atlantic Ocean	33,417,000	86,551,000
Indian Ocean	28,348,000	73,422,000
Arctic Ocean	5,105,000	13,223,000
South China Sea	1,149,000	2,975,000
Caribbean Sea	917,000	2,516,000
Mediterranean Sea	969,000	2,509,000
Bering Sea	873,000	2,261,000

FORMATION OF OCEANS

THE ATMOSPHERE FORMS
The semimolten surface of the Earth was covered by volcanoes. Hot gases and water vapor emitted by volcanoes formed the Earth's early atmosphere.

THE RAINS FALL
The water vapor in this early atmosphere condensed as rain. Rainstorms poured down on the planet and filled the vast hollows on the Earth's surface.

THE OCEANS FORM
These huge pools became the oceans. The water was hot and acidic. Later, plant life evolved and modified the chemical composition of the atmosphere and oceans.

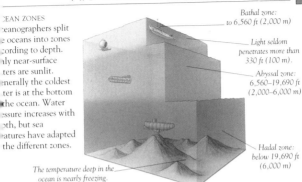

OCEAN ZONES
Oceanographers split the oceans into zones according to depth. Only near-surface waters are sunlit. Generally the coldest water is at the bottom of the ocean. Water pressure increases with depth, but sea temperatures have adapted to the different zones.

Bathal zone: to 6,560 ft (2,000 m)

Light seldom penetrates more than 330 ft (100 m).

Abyssal zone: 6,560–19,690 ft (2,000–6,000 m)

Hadal zone: below 19,690 ft (6,000 m)

The temperature deep in the ocean is nearly freezing.

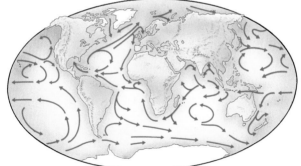

THE OCEANS' CURRENTS
Currents may be warm or cold. They flow across the surface or deep beneath it. The wind controls surface currents, which flow in circular directions. Currents carry some of the Sun's heat around the planet, warming polar areas and cooling tropical areas.

KEY	
COLD CURRENT	→
WARM CURRENT	→

WAVES AND TIDES

THE OCEANS AND seas are always moving. Buffeted by the wind and heated by the Sun, waves and currents form in the oceans. Ripples on the surface of the water may grow into waves that pound the shore and shape the coastlines. The Moon's and Sun's gravity pull the oceans, causing a daily and monthly cycle of tides.

WHIRLPOOL
An uneven channel can cause several tidal flows to collide. The currents surge upward and rush into each other. Eddies and whirlpools form on the surface.

Bulges in the oceans appear to sweep around the globe as the Earth rotates.

MONTHLY TIDES
High and low tides occur on a daily or twice daily rhythm. Tides are greater (spring tides) or smaller (neap tides) twice each month. This tide range depends on the relative positions of the Moon, Sun, and Earth.

The Moon's gravity pulls the oceans.

The rotation of the Earth results in a high tide about every 12.5 hours in the open ocean.

Earth's spinning on its axis affects the tides.

SPRING TIDES
The alignment of the Sun, Earth, and Moon create spring tides.

NEAP TIDES
Opposing pulls of the Sun and Moon cause neap tides.

GULF STREAM

A current of warm water called the
Gulf Stream moves from the Gulf
of Mexico across the Atlantic,
bringing mild winter weather to
the western coasts of Europe.
Like a huge river at sea, the
Gulf Stream flows 100 miles
(150 km) a day. This current
or gyre is 37 miles (60 km) wide
and 2,000 ft (600 m) deep. As
the Gulf Stream nears Europe, it is
called the "North Atlantic Drift."

NORTH
AMERICA

EUROPE

*Gulf
Stream*

GULF OF
MEXICO

*The warm water
slows and spreads out
as it nears Europe.*

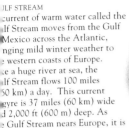

The top part of the wave,
the crest, continues up
the beach.

Particles near the surface
turn over and over

The beach slows
down the base of
the wave.

WAVE MOVEMENT

Waves travel toward the
shore from large storms
at sea. But it is not the
water particles that
travel, only the wave
form. The particles
rotate as each wave
passes and return to their
original position.

WAVE FACTS

• The highest recorded
wave was seen in the
western Pacific. It was
112 ft (34 m) high from
trough to crest.

• The Antarctic
Circumpolar Current
flows at a rate of
4.3 billion ft³ (130
million m³) per second.

• Hawaiian tides rise
2 in (45 cm) a day.

COMPOSITION OF
SEAWATER

The oceans contain
dissolved minerals,
some washed from
the land by rivers.
The predominant
constituents of
seawater are sodium
and chloride which
together form salt.
About 3.5 percent
of the weight of
ocean water is salt.

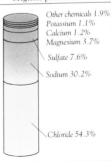

Other chemicals 1.9%
Potassium 1.1%
Calcium 1.2%
Magnesium 3.7%

Sulfate 7.6%

Sodium 30.2%

Chloride 54.3%

THE OCEAN FLOOR

THE WORLD UNDER the oceans has both strange and familiar features. Similar to a landscape on dry ground, mountains, valleys, and volcanoes dot the ocean floor. Once scientists had equipment to explore the ocean bed, they discovered that tectonic plate movement had caused many ocean floor features, including trenches, seamounts, and submarine canyons.

MAPPING THE OCEA
Oceanographers use
precision echo-
sounding, which
bounces signals off
ocean bed, to map
ocean floor's contou

FEATURES OF THE OCEAN FLOOR

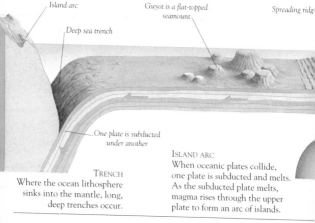

Island arc

Guyot is a flat-topped seamount

Spreading ridg

Deep sea trench

One plate is subducted under another

TRENCH
Where the ocean lithosphere sinks into the mantle, long, deep trenches occur.

ISLAND ARC
When oceanic plates collide, one plate is subducted and melts. As the subducted plate melts, magma rises through the upper plate to form an arc of islands.

DEEP-SEA EXPLORATION

DIVERS AND VEHICLES	DEPTH IN FEET	DEPTH IN METERS
Sponge diver holding breath	49	15
Air/SCUBA sports diver	164	50
Oil rig divers with diving bell	820	250
Deepest experimental dive	1,640	500
Barton's benthoscope	4,494	1,370
Cousteau diving saucer	11,000	3,350
Shinkai submersible	21,325	6,500
Trieste bathyscape	35,800	10,911

BATHYSCAPE
The deepest dive was made by the bathyscape *Trieste* in 1960. It dived in the world's deepest trench, the Mariana Trench.

SEAMOUNT
An underwater volcano that rises over 3,280 ft (1,000 m) is a seamount.

ABYSSAL PLAIN
This sediment-covered plain lies at a depth of about 15,000 ft (4,000 m).

SUBMARINE CANYON
Dense sediment flows from the continental shelf have eroded deep canyons.

Two of the Earth's tectonic plates are moving apart

Seamount

Submarine canyon

Continental shelf

Abyssal plain

Continental slope

Magma rises between the plates

Continental rise

MIDOCEANIC RIDGE
Magma rising between two tectonic plates forms a ridge.

CONTINENTAL SLOPE
The continental slope is the edge of the continent. It descends from the edge of the continental shelf to the rise, or into a trench.

CONTINENTAL SHELF
Stretching from the edge of the land like a vast plateau under the sea, the continental shelf averages 43 miles (70 km) wide. The ocean here is about 1,600 ft (250 m) deep.

OCEAN FEATURES

OCEANS ARE a rich source of many useful mineral substances. Seawater contains nutrients for phytoplankton and both metallic and nonmetallic minerals. Deposits of oil and gas are found in continental shelf sediment layers where tectonic paltes are rifting apart.

BLACK SMOKERS
In 1977, scientists discovered strange chimneys, formed from minerals on the ocean floor, called black smokers. In rift valleys between spreading ridges, they eject water as hot as 572°F (300°C), containing manganese and sulfur.

The vent minerals color the water black.

Smokers can grow as tall as 33 ft (10 m).

Jets of hot water shoot from the chimneys

Tubeworms and giant clams live on bacteria near the vents.

THE WORLD'S DEEPEST SEA TRENCHES

Trench	Depth in Feet	Depth in Meters
Mariana Trench, West Pacific	35,827	10,920
Tonga Trench, South Pacific	35,433	10,800
Philippine Trench, West Pacific	32,995	10,057
Kermadec Trench, South Pacific	37,963	10,047
Izu-Ogasawara Trench, West Pacific	32,087	9,780

OCEAN PRODUCT FACT

• There are 0.000004 parts per million of gold in the ocean.

• It takes a million years for a manganese nodule to grow 0.08 in (2 mm) in diameter.

OCEAN PRODUCTS

MANGANESE
Nodules from the
seabed are used
in industry.

OIL
This is a non-
renewable fossil
fuel. It is pumped
from rocks in the
continental shelf.

Diamond

*Diamonds in gravel are
known as alluvial diamonds.*

SAND
Rock pounded by
waves becomes
sand. In volcanic
areas it is black.

CORAL
Like sand,
coral is found in
coastal waters.

DIAMONDS IN GRAVEL
Off the coasts of Africa and
Indonesia, diamonds can be found
in continental shelf gravels. Most
have been washed down by rivers
into the sea.

OCEAN FLOOR SEDIMENT
The continental shelf is covered with
sand, mud, and silt washed onto it from
rivers. In the deep ocean, the floor is
coated with ooze. This contains the
remains of dead marine life.

*Rock is carried
311 miles (500 km)
from the ridge over
5 million years.
Sediment gathers.*

*After 10 million years,
the rock has moved
farther from the ridge.
It is now covered with
thick sediment.*

*New rock erupted
from the mantle
at mid-ocean
ridges has no
sediment cover.*

ISLANDS

A PIECE OF LAND smaller than a continent and surrounded by water is called an island. Magma rising from volcanic vents in the oceanic lithosphere creates islands in the sea. An arc of islands appears where a tectonic plate is subducted. Some islands exist only when the tide is high; at low tide it is possible to walk to these islands. Small islands may exist in rivers and lakes. In warmer regions coral reefs may grow from the sea, built by living organisms.

Causeway

A narrow s
of land li
the island
the shore

CAUSEWAY
A change in sea level can create an island. Land may be accessible only at low tide by a causeway. At high tide the island is cut off.

ISLAND FACTS

• Bouvet Island is the most remote island – about 1,056 miles (1,700 km) from the nearest landmass (Antarctica).

• Kwejalein in the Marshall Islands, in the Pacific Ocean, is the largest coral atoll. Its reef measures 176 miles (283 km) long.

ISLAND ARC
On one side of a subduction zone, a curved chain arc of volcanic islands may be pushed up from un the ocean floor. From space, the numerous volcan peaks on the islands of Indonesia are clearly visib

THE WORLD'S LARGEST ISLANDS

ISLAND	AREA IN MILES ^{2}	AREA IN KM ^{2}
...enland	839,852	2,175,219
...v Guinea	305,981	792,493
...neo	280,083	725,416
...lagascar	226,644	587,009
...n Island, Canada	195,916	507,423
...natra , Indonesia	104,990	427,325
...nshu, Japan	87,799	227,401
...at Britain	84,195	218,065

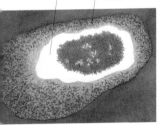

...d builds up more
...ne side of the reef.

New coral organisms grow on old coral skeletons.

...RAL
...nds such as the Maldives in the Indian
...ean are known as "coral." Tiny marine
...anisms called corals grow on submerged
...k formations such as undersea
... canoes (seamounts) in warm, salty seas.
...e coral grows slowly up to the ocean's
...face and, when the sea level drops,
...ates a firm platform above sea level.

FORMATION OF A CORAL ATOLL

Volcanic island

1 A FRINGING REEF
Where a volcano has emerged from under the ocean, coral begins to grow on its fringes, around the base of the volcano.

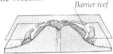

Barrier reef

2 A BARRIER REEF
When volcanic activity subsides, the peak erodes and sinks. The coral forms a reef around the edge of the volcano.

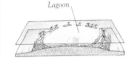

Lagoon

3 AN ATOLL FORMS
Eventually, the volcano sinks beneath the sea. A ring of coral known as an atoll remains on the surface.

COASTS

WHERE THE LAND meets the sea there is the coast
Coasts may be bordered by cliffs, dunes, or pebble
beaches. There is a continual battle between sea
and coast as rock is broken down by pounding
waves, and sand is carried about by wind. Some
coasts retreat, but new coast is always being
created in other areas. Beache
alter their height and width
with the seasons.

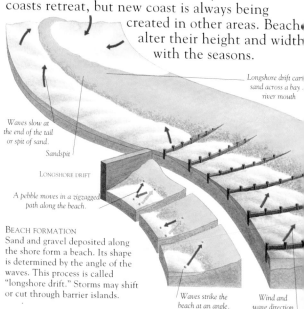

*Longshore drift car
sand across a bay
river mouth*

*Waves slow at
the end of the tail
or spit of sand.*

Sandspit

LONGSHORE DRIFT

*A pebble moves in a zigzagged
path along the beach.*

BEACH FORMATION
Sand and gravel deposited along
the shore form a beach. Its shape
is determined by the angle of the
waves. This process is called
"longshore drift." Storms may shift
or cut through barrier islands.

*Waves strike the
beach at an angle.*

*Wind and
wave direction*

The largest pleasure
each is Virginia Beach,
ith an area of
0 miles² (803 km²).

The world has about
12,000 miles (504,000
m) of coastline.

The highest sea cliffs
re at Molokai, Hawaii.
hey descend 3,300 ft
,010 m) to the sea.

At Martha's Vineyard,
ass., the cliffs retreat
6 ft (1.7 m) per year.

*Groynes, or fences,
built into the sea prevent
longshore drift.*

*Sand builds up
against the
groin.*

d and shingle

TYPES OF COAST

*Direction
of waves*

TOMBOLO
This type of coastline
links an island to the
shore by a strip of sand.

BARRIER BEACH
A lagoon forms behind
a barrier of sand built
by onshore waves.

*Direction of
waves*

BAYHEAD BEACH
Waves striking a head-
land at an angle leave
a protected arc of sand.

FJORD COASTLINE
A submerged glacial
valley with steep sides
forms a fjord coastline.

SEA STACKS
Waves, carrying
sand and pebbles,
gradually wear away
a headland. First, a
cave appears, which
is enlarged to form
an arch. Then, the
arch falls, leaving
an isolated stack.

*Sea cave eroded
by sea until
arch forms*

*Top of arch
collapses leaving
pillar or stack*

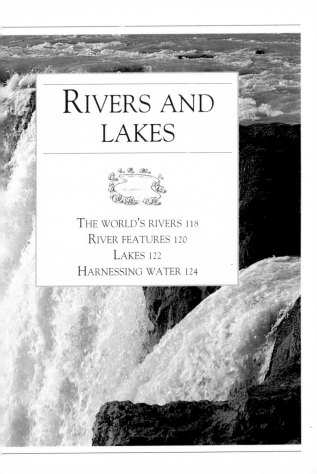

RIVERS AND LAKES

THE WORLD'S RIVERS

WHEREVER THEY occur, rivers are a key part of the Earth's water cycle. They carry snowmelt and rainwater from high areas down to the sea, filling up marshes and lakes where the land surface is uneven. In arid regions small rivers may be intermittent. They dry up and reappear after heavy rains or during an annual wet season.

PERENNIAL RIVER
In temperate and tropical areas a reliable supply of rainwater create perennial rivers. Rivers such as th Nile, in Africa, flow all year.

THE WATER CYCLE
Water is constantly cycling between land, sea, and air. The Sun's heat causes evaporation from seas, lakes, or rivers. Water vapor rises and cools. Tiny droplets of water condense and form clouds. The drops grow and eventually fall as rain.

Rain and snow fall on high ground.

On land, water vapor released by plants and so

RIVER FACTS
• The Nile River is longer, but the Amazon carries more water.

• China's Yangtze carries 1,600,000 tons (tonnes) of silt a year.

Water seeps underground and flows to the sea.

Water evaporates from sea and lakes to form clouds of water vapor.

Riv flow the

ASONAL RIVER
is dry riverbed belongs to a
anish river. In the hot
mmer, many rivers dry up, but
n will fill them up during the
t winter season.

THE WORLD'S LONGEST RIVERS

RIVER AND CONTINENT	LENGTH IN MILES	LENGTH IN KM
Nile, Africa	4,160	6,695
Amazon, S. America	4,000	6,437
Yangtze/Chang Jiang, Asia	3,964	6,379
Mississippi-Missouri, N. America	3,892	6,264
Ob-Irtysh, Asia	3,362	5,411
Yellow/Huang He, Asia	2,903	4,672
Congo/Zaire, Africa	2,897	4,662
Amur, Asia	2,744	4,416
Lena, Asia	2,734	4,400
Mackenzie-Peace, N. America	2,635	4,241

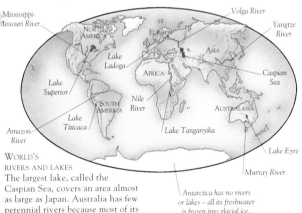

Mississippi-Missouri River

Volga River

NORTH AMERICA

EUROPE

ASIA

Yangtze River

Lake Ladoga

AFRICA

Caspian Sea

Lake Superior

SOUTH AMERICA

Nile River

AUSTRALASIA

Lake Titicaca

Amazon River

Lake Tanganyika

Lake Eyre

Murray River

**WORLD'S
RIVERS AND LAKES**
The largest lake, called the
Caspian Sea, covers an area almost
as large as Japan. Australia has few
perennial rivers because most of its
land area is desert.

Antarctica has no rivers
or lakes – all its freshwater
is frozen into glacial ice.

RIVER FEATURES

FROM ITS SOURCE in the mountains, the snow or rainwater that fills a stream cuts a path through sediment and bedrock on its way to the sea. Streams join and form a river that flows more slowly, meandering across the land. A river may carry a large amount of sediment, which it deposits on its floodplain or in a delta.

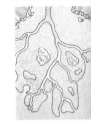

DELTA
At the river's mouth it sheds its sediment to form a broad fan of swampy land.

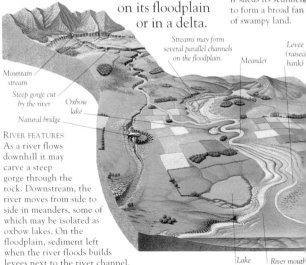

Mountain stream

Steep gorge cut by the river

Natural bridge

Oxbow lake

Streams may form several parallel channels on the floodplain.

Meander

Levee (raised bank)

Lake

River mouth

RIVER FEATURES
As a river flows downhill it may carve a steep gorge through the rock. Downstream, the river moves from side to side in meanders, some of which may be isolated as oxbow lakes. On the floodplain, sediment left when the river floods builds levees next to the river channel.

MELTWATER
A river may begin its life in a glaciated part of the world. Melting ice and snow from a glacier feed mountain streams.

OVERLAND FLOW
Rainwater running downhill gathers into small streams called "tributaries," which join to form a river.

SPRING
A rock layer called the "aquifer" stores rainwater. Springs form where streams cut into aquifer rock layers.

MORE RIVER FACTS
• The Ganges and Brahmaputra delta, India, is the largest in the world. Its area is about 30,000 miles^2 (75,000 km^2).

• The widest waterfall is Khone Falls in Laos. They are 6.7 miles (10.8 km) wide.

• Each year rivers unload 20 billion tons (tonnes) of sediment into the sea.

Softer rock undercut by erosion

Swirling rocks and water

Hard rock

Floodplain where sediment is deposited

Most rivers run into the sea

Sediment on seabed

WATERFALLS
A river flows swiftly near its source, cutting through soft rocks more easily than hard. A sheer face of hard rock is exposed where water plunges, undercutting the rock below.

THE WORLD'S HIGHEST WATERFALLS

WATERFALL AND COUNTRY	HEIGHT IN FEET	HEIGHT IN METERS
Angel Falls, Venezuela	3,212	979
Tugela Falls, S. Africa	2,799	853
Utgaard, Norway	2,625	800
Mongefossen, Norway	2,539	774
Yosemite Falls, US	2,425	739

LAKES

AN INLAND BODY of freshwater or brackish water, collected in a basin, is called a "lake." In geological terms, lakes are short-lived; they can dry up or become clogged in a few thousand years. Lakes form when depressions resulting from lithosphere movement, erosion, or volcanic craters fill up with water. The Caspian Sea, the world's largest lake, and Lake Baikal, Siberia, the deepest lake, were both produced when shifts of the lithosphere cut off large arms of the sea.

SWAMP
The Everglades, Florida, are mangrove swamps. In warm climates, mangrove trees grow in the salty (brackish) water of muddy estuaries. The trees form islands in the mud.

TYPES OF LAKE

KETTLE LAKE
Ice left behind by a melting glacier may be surrounded by moraine. When the ice melts the depression forms a kettle lake.

TARN
A circular mountain lake is known as a tarn. These lakes form in hollows worn by glacial erosion or blocked by ice debris.

VOLCANIC LAKE
The craters of ancient volcanoes fill up with water and produce lakes such as Crater Lake, Oregon.

VANISHING LAKES

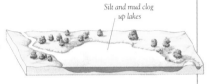

Silt and mud clog up lakes

SEDIMENT BUILDS

Lakes begin to fill up with sediment, washed into them by rivers. The mud and silt create a delta in the lake, which has areas of dry land.

Channels become narrow

SWAMP FORMS

The lake area gets smaller and shallower. Islands of dry land fan out into the lake. Reeds grow, turning the lake into a swamp.

LAKE DISAPPEARS

Eventually, the lake area is colonized by plants, forming a wetland environment.

Plants grow in the sediment

OXBOW LAKE

This curved lake appears when a river cuts off a meander loop. Eventually, the isolated lake fills with sediment and vegetation.

THE WORLD'S LARGEST LAKES AND INLAND SEAS

LAKE AND CONTINENT	AREA IN MILES²	AREA IN KM²
Caspian Sea, Asia/ Europe	143,236	370,980
Lake Superior, N. America	31,698	82,098
Lake Victoria, Africa	26,826	69,480
Lake Huron, N. America	22,999	59,566
Lake Michigan, N. America	22,299	57,754
Aral Sea, Asia	14,307	37,056
Lake Tanganyika, Africa	12,699	32,891
Lake Baikal, Asia	12,161	31,498
Great Bear Lake, N. America	12,045	31,197

HARNESSING WATER

HUMANS CANNOT survive without freshwater. It is necessary for human consumption, crops, and industry. Rainwater is stored in reservoirs and aquifers for later use. River flow can be channeled to crop irrigation networks and into canals that allow barge traffic. Water's moving energy can be harnessed in hydroelectric power stations to produce electricity. For domestic use, water is cleansed, treated, and recycled.

IRRIGATION
Rice terracing is a method of crop irrigation used in Indonesia. Growing rice requires a great deal of water. To make maximum use of rainfall, a system of channels carries water to the fields of rice. The fields are cut in terraces down the hillsides.

CANALS
During the Industrial Revolution in Britain in the 1800s, a network of waterways called canals was constructed. Goods could be transported by barges that were pulled along by horses. Aqueducts carry canals and their traffic over obstacles.

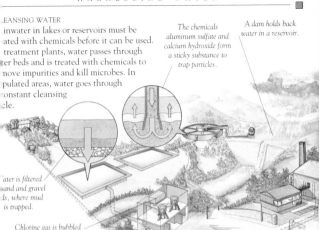

CLEANSING WATER

Rainwater in lakes or reservoirs must be treated with chemicals before it can be used. In treatment plants, water passes through filter beds and is treated with chemicals to remove impurities and kill microbes. In populated areas, water goes through a constant cleansing cycle.

The chemicals aluminum sulfate and calcium hydroxide form a sticky substance to trap particles.

A dam holds back water in a reservoir.

Water is filtered in sand and gravel beds, where mud is trapped.

Chlorine gas is bubbled through the water to kill bacteria.

DAMS

A dammed river, like this one in California, can be used to produce hydroelectric power. Water held in a reservoir by a dam turns a turbine that is linked to an electrical generator. In the same way, river water above a waterfall can be diverted to power turbine generators.

DAM FACTS

• Water held by Volta Dam in Ghana could flood 3,282 miles^2 (8,500 km^2).

• A chain of dams being built along the Amazon could flood an area the size of England.

• There are more than 200 dams around the world that are over 492 ft (150 m) tall.

CLIMATE AND WEATHER

CLIMATE

TYPICAL LONG-TERM weather conditions for an area a
known as its "climate." The three broad climate zone
are tropical, temperate, and polar. One factor that
affects climate is distance from the equator (latitude
Different areas of the planet at the same latitude sha
the same climate. The nearer the equator the
warmer the climate; the nearer the poles
the colder. Distance from the sea and
altitude also affect climate.

TEMPERATE GRASSLAND
The temperate climates of
North America and
Northern Europe
experience seasonal
change but similar
monthly rainfall all year.

MICROCLIMATE
In a city, such as Paris, the
weather may differ from that
of outlying areas. Roads and
buildings absorb heat to
create a local, or microclimate.

TROPICAL RAINFOREST
Regions of dense vegetation near the
equator have a climate that is hot and
wet all year round. The temperature stays
constant at about 80–82°F (27–28°C).

POLAR REGIONS AND TUNDRA REGIONS

At the ice-covered poles, temperatures only rise above freezing for a few months of the year. The cold, dry tundra region surrounds the North Pole.

CLIMATE FACTS

• The temperature in the shade at al'Aziziyah, Libya, 136°F (58°C), is the highest recorded.

• Oymyakon in Siberia, the coldest inhabited place, can reach –90° F (–68°C).

MOUNTAIN REGIONS

The temperature falls the higher up a mountain you go. Trees and plants grow on the low slopes, but little grows above the snowline.

MAP OF CLIMATIC ZONES

HOT DESERT

Few animals and plants can live in the hot, dry conditions of the desert. The temperature can reach 100°F (38°C) and it may not rain for several years.

KEY TO CLIMATIC ZONES

- Polar
- Tundra
- Mountain
- Temperate grassland
- Tropical rainforest
- Hot desert

WIND AND WEATHER

WINDS CIRCULATE air around the planet. They carry warm air from the equator to the poles and cold air in the opposite direction. This process balances the Earth's temperature. Some global winds (known as prevailing winds), such as polar easterlies and trade winds, are an important part of the world's weather systems.

Cold polar easterl sink and spread t warmer areas.

Warm rises spre ove cold

Prevailing winds in temperate regions of the Northern Hemisphere blow from the southwest.

Trade winds

There is very little wind in the doldrums on the equator.

Hot air moves away from the equator toward the poles, where it cools.

Prevailing winds in temperate regions of the Southern Hemisphere blow from the northwest.

Cold polar air

Cells of circulate ab the pla

WIND FACTS

• In Antarctica wind can reach speeds of 200 mph (320 km/h).

• Highest wind speed recorded at ground level is 230 mph (371 km/h).

WINDS OF THE WORLD

Three prevailing winds blow around the planet at ground level, on either side of the equator. Trade win bring dry weather, westerly winds are damp and warm and polar easterlies carry dry, cold, polar air.

FORMATION OF A ROSSBY WAVE

A SNAKING WIND
The Earth's rotation causes curling, high altitude winds called Rossby waves.

DEEPENING WAVE
The wave deepens along the polar front. It forms a meander 1,250 miles (2,000 km) long.

DEVELOPED LOOPS
The curls become loops and the hot and cold air separate to produce swirling frontal storms.

Earth's rotation deflects winds on the ground.

Trade winds near the equator

RADE WINDS
the area on either side of the quator (the tropics) the evailing winds are called the rade winds." In the northern emisphere, the winds blow om the northeast, and in the uthern hemisphere they ow from the southeast.

SEA BREEZES AND LAND BREEZES
On sunny days, the land warms up during the day. Warm air rises from the land and cool air is drawn in from the sea. At night, the land cools down quickly and cold air sinks out to sea.

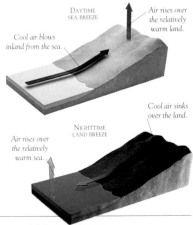

DAYTIME SEA BREEZE

Air rises over the relatively warm land.

Cool air blows inland from the sea.

Cool air sinks over the land.

NIGHTTIME LAND BREEZE

Air rises over the relatively warm sea.

WEATHER MAPPING

MILLIONS OF PEOPLE listen to the
weather forecast each day. The
forecast is compiled using data
collected from all around the world
and from weather satellites in
space. Meteorologists study the
movements of warm and cold air
masses and the fronts where they
meet. Using this information,
they plot weather charts and
predict the coming weather.

SATELLITE IMAGES
From space, Earth appea
to be surrounded by
clouds. This image show
clouds over the Caribbea

WEATHER MAP
A picture of the
weather at a given
time can be shown
on a weather map,
known as a "synoptic
chart." Standard
symbols are used, such
as lines to show fronts
(where one body of
air – an air mass –
meets another).

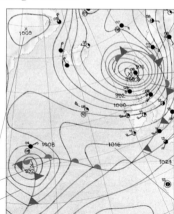

Occluded fro
– merged war
and cold fron

A depression
a center of lo
pressure.

Closer isoba
indicate
stronger win

Shows wind
strength and
direction

Cold front –
cold air is
advancing.

Air pressure i
millibars

Center of high pressure

Warm front – warm
air is advancing

Isobars link points with
the same air pressure.

FORMATION OF A DEPRESSION

AIR MASSES

Air masses are vast areas of wet or dry, warm or cold air. At the polar front, a warm air mass and a cold one collide.

FORMING A BULGE

The warm tropical air mass pushes into the cold polar air along the polar front. The front begins to bulge.

DIVIDING INTO TWO

The Earth's rotation spins the air masses. Cold air pursues warm air in a spiral formation. The polar front splits.

OCCLUDED FRONT

When the cold front catches up with the warm front, it pushes under the warm air. An occluded front results.

WEATHER FACTS

• A cold front can advance at up to 30 mph (50 km/h) and may overtake a warm front.

• The first television weather chart was broadcast in Britain on November 11, 1936.

• An air mass can cover an area as large as Brazil.

BAROMETER

The air around the Earth has mass and exerts pressure. A barometer measures air pressure in units called "millibars."

TEMPERATURE PEAKS

Troughs in the temperature graph show when ice sheets advanced to cover high latitude and land masses. These cold periods were separated by interglacials when the average temperature rose and the ice sheets retreated.

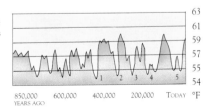

850,000	600,000	400,000	200,000	TODAY	°F

YEARS AGO

63
61
59
57
55
54

CLOUDS

AIR RISES as it warms, as it passes over mountains, or as it is pushed over air masses near the ground. Rising air cools, water vapor condenses, and forms clouds of water droplets. There are three cloud levels: cirrus form at the highest level, alto in the middle, and stratus at the lowest level.

FOGGY AIR
Clouds that form at ground level are known as "fog." Fog, mixed with smoke from burning fuels, produces smog. Earlier this century, London, England, suffered from severe smog.

CLOUD FORMATION

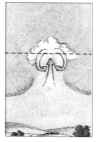

THE LAND WARMS
The Sun warms the land on a clear day. Air near the ground is warmed and rises.

A CLOUD FORMS
As the warm air rises, it cools. The moisture it contains condenses and forms a cloud.

GROWING CLOUDS
Fleecy clouds appear in the sky. They get bigger and cool air circulates inside them.

SKY COVERAGE

The amount of cloud cover is shown on weather maps by a circle with one of these symbols

CLEAR   1   2

3   4   5   6   7   8

Freezing level

A
B
C
D
E
F
G
H
I

CLOUD TYPES

CIRRUS (A)
• wisps of cloud made of ice crystals
• about 39,372 ft (12, 000 m) high

CIRROCUMULUS (B)
• forms at about 29,529 ft (9,000 m)
• rippled ice crystal cloud

CUMULONIMBUS (C)
• dark, storm cloud with large vertical development

ALTOCUMULUS (D)
• layers or rolls of fluffy cloud

ALTOSTRATUS (E)
• gray or white sheet of cloud
• forms between 6,562 ft and 19,685 ft (2,000 m and 6,000 m)

STRATOCUMULUS (F)
• layer at the top of cumulus cloud

CUMULUS (G)
• large, heaped white fluffy cloud

NIMBOSTRATUS (H)
• low, rain cloud
• under 6,562 ft (2,000 m)

STRATUS (I)
• low-level, flat gray sheet of cloud

RAIN AND THUNDERSTORMS

EARTH'S WATER CYCLE relies on rain. Rain fills rivers and lakes and provides water for plants and animals. T water droplets in the air form rain when they gather in larger drops inside clouds. Raindrops can be moved around by air currents. L rain or snowfall may come from altostratus clouds, heavy rain fr stratus clouds, and torrential rains, or thunderstorms, from cumulonimbus clou

Droplets of more than 0.2 in (0.5 mm) fall as rain.

Smaller drops of water fall as drizzle.

Rising air

HOW RAIN FORMS
In warm regions, rising air currents agitate the water droplets in clouds until they join into raindrops. In temperate regions, ice crystals in the clouds above freezing level melt on their way down and form rain.

MONSOON
Seasonal winds called "summer monsoons" draw moist air inland, bringing rain to southern Asia. In winter, a cold, dry wind (winter monsoon) blows over land and out to sea.

RAIN FACTS

A record 73.62 in (1,870 mm) of rain fell in one month in 1861 in Cherrapunji, India.

Tutunendo, Colombia, the world's wettest place, has an annual rainfall of 463.4 in (11,770 mm).

LIGHTNING

Turbulence and collision of ice particles and water droplets inside a storm may cause electric charges. Positive charges gather at the top of the cloud and negative ones at the base. When the electricity is released it flashes between clouds or sparks to the ground and back.

Positive charges

Negative charges

RAINBOWS

Sunlight striking raindrops is refracted, reflected by the backs of the droplets, and refracted again. This causes the white light to split into its seven constituent colors: red, orange, yellow, green, blue, indigo, and violet.

RAINFALL MAP

Around the world, rainfall varies greatly. Warm seas in the tropics evaporate and bring lots of rain. Near the sea, land is wetter, but mountains may block rain.

KEY TO ANNUAL RAINFALL

- Less than 10 in (250 mm)
- 10–20 in (250–500 mm)
- 20–39 in (500–1,000 mm)
- 39–79 in (1,000–2,000 mm)
- 79–118 in (2,000–3,000 mm)
- More than 118 in (3,000 mm)

SNOW, HAIL, AND SLEET

WHEN THE WEATHER is very cold, snow, hail, or sleet leave a white coating on the landscape. Snow and hail result from water freezing in the clouds. Snow falls from the altostratus clouds, and hail from thunderstorm clouds. Sleet forms when partially frozen rainwater freezes completely as it touches any cold surface.

SNOWY WEATHER
In the European Alps, the snow the winter months does not me because the ground temperature low. Strong winds sometimes bl the snow into deep snowdrifts.

HOW SNOW FORMS
High up in the atmosphere, above the freezing level, water droplets in clouds form ice crystals, which collide and combine. As they fall, the ice crystals form snowflakes or hail.

SNOW FACTS

• The largest recorded hailstone weighed 1.7 lb (765 g) and fell in Kansas in 1970.

• In 1921, 76 in (1,930 mm) of snow fell in Colorado in one day.

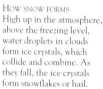

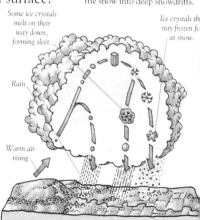

Some ice crystals melt on their way down, forming sleet.

Ice crystals th stay frozen f as snow.

Rain

Warm air rising

r currents toss ice
crystals around.

*Hailstones have
alternate layers of
clear and opaque ice.*

e crystals
freeze at
top of the
cloud.

Rising air

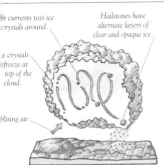

OW HAIL FORMS
cumulonimbus clouds above 6 miles
0 km) the temperature is freezing. Water
oplets blown to the top of the cloud freeze.
yers of ice build up around the hailstone
t repeatedly melts and refreezes in its
otion through the cloud.

ICICLES

Spectacular ice shapes such as
icicles form when water freezes in
cold weather. Icicles grow as drips
of melting snow or ice refreeze.

*The outside of an
icicle freezes
before the inside.*

*Icicles often
hang from
leaking pipes.*

HOARFROST

Below freezing point, water
vapor in the air freezes. It
leaves spiky crystals of
hoarfrost on cold surfaces.

OZEN RIVER
e Zanskar River in the Himalayas is frozen
ring the winter months. The frozen river makes
aveling in the region easier, since local people
n walk up and down the stream on the ice. Under
e ice, fish can survive in the unfrozen water.
summer, the river is a fast-flowing torrent.

HURRICANES AND TORNADOES

FIERCE WINDS such as hurricanes and tornadoes occur when warm air masses encounter cold air masses. Winds reach high speeds and bring torrential rain and huge dark clouds. A tornado concentrates its havoc on a fairly narrow trail whereas a hurricane destroys a much larger area and can last for many days.

BEAUFORT SCALE

NUMBER	DESCRIPTION
0	Calm, smoke rises straight up
1	Light air, smoke drifts gently
2	Light breeze, leaves rustle
3	Gentle breeze, flags flutter
4	Moderate wind, twigs move
5	Fresh wind, small trees sway
6	Strong wind, large branches move
7	Near gale, whole tree sways
8	Gale, difficult to walk in wind
9	Severe wind, slates and branches break
10	Storm, houses damaged, trees blown down
11	Severe storm, buildings seriously damaged
12	Hurricane, devastating damage

SATELLITE PHOTOGRAPH
Hurricanes can be tracked easily using hurricane hunter planes and weather satellites. The small central eye develops as the hurricane reaches full intensity.

HURRICANE
Low-lying coasts are endangered by the high winds that generate large waves and also push water onshore as a destructive storm surge.

...rus and
...ostratus
...ds around
edge of
storm.

...urricanes
...n be as wide
...480 miles
...800 km).

Bands of wind
and rain spiral.

At the eye,
the sky is
clear and
winds light.

Currents rise
and spread
outward.

HOW A HURRICANE FORMS

A cluster of tropical storms can become a hurricane. Bands of cumulonimbus and cumulus clouds spiral toward the center of the storm. Warm air rises and cools, building huge storm clouds that bring rain. At the center, or eye, of the hurricane, the pressure is low and the weather is calm.

WATERSPOUT

...a tornado occurs over
...e ocean it is known as
...aterspout. Water
...ray from the sea swirls
...ound the base of the
...out. The water vapor
...gher up condenses in a
...irling tubular cloud.

A violent
updraft sucks
up soil and
debris.

Winds in the
tornado may
reach speeds of
200 mph
(320 km/h).

HURRICANE FACTS

• Winds up to 100 mph
(160 km/h) have been
...ecorded in a hurricane.

• Hurricanes spin
...ounterclockwise north
...f the equator and clock-
...ise south of the
...quator.

• Waterspouts are
...sually between
...64 and 330 ft
...50–100 m) high.

TORNADO

If a mass of cool, dry air collides with a mass of warm, damp air it may form a squall line of tornado-generating thunderstorms. The storm may last only a few minutes, but its spinning winds are very destructive. Tornados are most frequent in the Midwestern US.

A FUTURE FOR THE EARTH

ECOLOGY

THE STUDY OF the relationships between animals and plants, and between them and their environment, is called "ecology." Ecology explains how individual species fit into the natural world. Ecologists study how organisms obtain food and materials to survive and the effect this has on the environment and on other organisms. Ernst Haekel, a German biologist, first used the term "ecology" in 1866.

ECOSYSTEMS
Several communities of living thing their physical surroundings, and the climate make up an ecosystem. Bea forest, and ocean communities are examples of ecosystems.

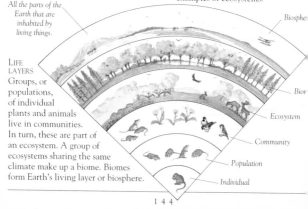

All the parts of the Earth that are inhabited by living things.

Biosphe

LIFE LAYERS
Groups, or populations, of individual plants and animals live in communities. In turn, these are part of an ecosystem. A group of ecosystems sharing the same climate make up a biome. Biomes form Earth's living layer or biosphere.

Bior

Ecosystem

Community

Population

Individual

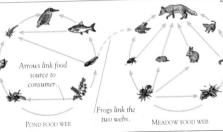

OD WEB

ding relationships
ween organisms in
ecosystem can be
nplex. Energy, as
d, is transferred
ng a chain from
ts to herbivores
arnivores. Chains
erconnect to build
od web.

*Arrows link food
source to
consumer.*

*Frogs link the
two webs.*

POND FOOD WEB   MEADOW FOOD WEB

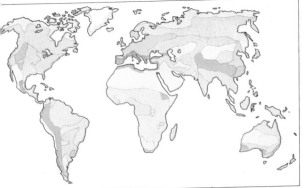

E WORLD'S BIOMES

ch zone or biome on the map
ove is distinguished by its
nate and other physical
tures. The conditions in each
me support particular plants
l animals. Biomes form in
ads roughly parallel to the
es of latitude.

KEY FOR BIOMES MAP

○ Tundra   ○ Temperate rainforest
○ Boreal forest   ○ Scrubland
○ Mountain   ○ Desert
○ Temperate grassland ○ Tropical rainforest
○ Temperate forest   ○ Savanna

HABITAT DESTRUCTION

AS HUMANS SEEK a more comfortable life, the Earth's resources are being used up or destroyed. Fossil fuels are burned to provide energy, and waste is dumped, which pollutes land, sea, and air. Toxins that do not break down are left to poison the planet. Cultivating more and more land has led to the loss of habitats like the rain forest, endangering its many unique species. We need to protect the Earth – our own habitat for our own survival.

DEFORESTATION
Forests are destroyed as people clear land for their animals, to grow crops, or to sell the wood. Deforestation leads to habitat and wildlife loss.

Oil spilled at sea is washed up on the beach.

WATER POLLUTION
Once in the water cycle, pollutants such as chemical waste, gasoline, or oil can contaminate surface and ground water. Pollution of oceans and beaches kills animals and plants and poisons their habitats.

DESERTIFICATION
Deserts are growing because of climate change and overgrazing, which cause soil erosion.

[AC]ID RAIN

[Tre]es in Europe and [N]orth America suffer [da]mage by acid rain. [Su]lfur dioxide is [rel]eased into the air [wh]en fossil fuels are [bur]ned. This mixes [wit]h rainwater to [pr]oduce a weak [sul]furic acid, which [kil]ls areas of forest.

Ozone hole shown in purple on this satellite image

POLLUTION FACTS

• The temperature on Earth could rise by 7°F (4°C) by the year 2050.

• A 3.3 ft (1 m) rise in sea level could flood 310,694 miles (500,000 km) of coastline.

• Each CFC molecule can destroy 100,000 molecules of ozone.

• An area of rain forest the size of a soccer field is destroyed every second.

OZONE HOLE

The ozone layer blocks out most of the Sun's harmful ultraviolet radiation. Leakage of CFCs (chlorofluorocarbons), used in refrigerators, packaging, and aerosols, may be causing a hole in the ozone layer over Antarctica.

More heat is reflected back to Earth.

Less heat escapes

Gases trapped in Earth's atmosphere

Surface of the Earth gets hotter.

[GL]OBAL WARMING

[Po]lluting gases such as carbon dioxide [ac]cumulate in the Earth's atmosphere. [The]se gases, also known as greenhouse gases, [pre]vent heat from escaping from the surface of [th]e planet and cause the temperature on Earth [to] rise, a process called "global warming."

CONSERVATION

ENDANGERED wildlife can benefit from our attempts to protect the environment. Animals and plants need their habitats preserved. Some endangered animal and plant species need the protection provided only by zoos and botanical gardens. Less waste and less pollution will also protect our unique planet.

CAPTIVE BREEDING
Endangered species, such as pandas, are encouraged to breed in captivity. This practice helps maintain and increase animal numbers.

ADAPTING TO CHANGE
Animals such as foxes and raccoons have adapted to increased urbanization. Many now live in parks and gardens and scavenge for food in trash cans.

Foxes are a familiar sight in gardens.

WILDLIFE RESERVES
One species becomes extinct every day through hunting or habitat destruction. However, in some parts of the world, animals such as rhinos, zebras, and elephants are protected in wildlife reserves where they can live and breed in a protected and natural environment.

RECYCLING TRASH

An average family throws away two tons (tonnes) of trash every year. A large proportion of household waste such as organic matter, glass, paper, metal, and some plastics, all have good recycling potential. The remaining trash is still deposited in a diminishing number of land fills.

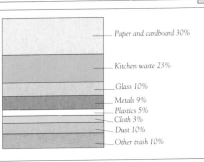

Paper and cardboard 30%

Kitchen waste 23%

Glass 10%

Metals 9%

Plastics 5%

Cloth 3%

Dust 10%

Other trash 10%

LAST WILDERNESS

Frozen Antarctica is a nearly deserted land, but the sea around it is teeming with life. Toxic dumping and mining are banned by an international convention in order to preserve Antarctica as Earth's last wilderness.

CONSERVATION FACTS

• Ingredients in some medicines, chocolate, and chewing gum were originally discovered in the rainforest.

• The bald eagle is no longer endangered because of breeding programs and protection laws.

• In 2000, 1.27 percent of California's electricity was generated by wind turbines.

FUTURE ENERGY

Fossil fuels that are burned to provide electricity will eventually run out. The Sun is a possible alternative energy source. Electric cars with solar panels are not practical but solar-powered telephones are already in use in some sunnier parts of the world.

Glossary

ABYSSAL PLAIN
A sediment-covered plain on the ocean floor.

ACID RAIN
Rain that is acidic due to pollution by sulfur dioxide and other gases.

ANTICYCLONE
Area of high atmospheric pressure.

ASTHENOSPHERE
Semimolten mantle layer that lies beneath the lithosphere.

ATMOSPHERE
Envelope of air that surrounds the Earth. It can be divided into four layers: troposphere, stratosphere, mesosphere, and thermosphere.

ATOLL
A circular line of coral islands around a lagoon.

AVALANCHE
A rapid movement of unstable snow, ice, or rock down a mountain slope.

BAROMETER
An instrument that measures atmospheric pressure.

BASALT
The most common extrusive igneous rock. It is fine-grained and varies from dark gray to black in color.

BEACH
Strip of loose sediment that lies between the cliffs or dunes and the lowest tides.

BEAUFORT SCALE
A twelve-step scale using observations of ocean waves, flags, and smoke to gauge wind velocity.

BIOSPHERE
Layer where life is found on Earth.

BLACK SMOKER
Chimneylike vent on a rift-valley floor from which black, mineral-rich hot water gushes.

BRECCIA
Sedimentary rock composed of coarse, angular rock fragments held together by a mineral cement.

CANYON
A deep valley with almost vertical sides, eroded by a river.

CFC
Chlorofluorocarbon containing carbon, chlorine, and fluorine. It is used in aerosol sprays, packaging, and refrigerators.

CIRRUS CLOUD
An ice-crystal cloud that forms in the upper troposphere.

CLEAVAGE
A well-defined plane along which a mineral tends to break, related to weakness in the atomic structure of the mineral.

CLIMATE
The average weather conditions for a region over a long period of time.

CONTACT METAMORPHISM
Baking and mineral change in rock near a magma chamber or in contact with dikes, sills, or lava flows.

CONTINENTAL DRIFT
Theory suggesting that the Earth's continents have moved (drifted) relative to one another.

CORE
The Earth's center sphere of nickel-iron, with a molten outer shell and solid inner part.

CRUST
The upper rock zone of the lithosphere.

CUMULONIMBUS CLOUD
Tall convective cloud that often brings rain.

CUMULUS CLOUD
Fluffy cloud usually accompanying fine weather.

CYCLONE
An area of low atmospheric pressure. Also a hurricane.

DEFORESTATION
Cutting down trees and clearing forests for crops, lumber, and grazing land.

DESERTIFICATION
Creation of deserts by soil erosion through over-grazing, overcultivation, or overpopulation.

ECOLOGY
Study of interactions between living organisms and their environment.

ECOSYSTEM
Communities of animals and plants dependent on each other and their environment for survival.

ENVIRONMENT
The life forms and air, water, and soil conditions of an area.

EPICENTER
Point on the Earth's surface directly above the focus of an earthquake.

EROSION
The removal of soil and weathered rock by wind, flowing water, or glaciers.

ESTUARY
The drowned mouth of a river where freshwater mixes with ocean water.

EXTRUSIVE IGNEOUS ROCK
Rock formed from lava erupted from volcanoes.

FIRN
Old, dense, granular compacted snow.

FISSURE ERUPTION
Volcanic eruption from a crack or linear vent in the ground.

FJORD
A former glacial valley with steep sides and a U-shaped profile, that is now occupied by sea water.

FOCUS
Underground location where an earthquake originates.

FOSSIL
Remains or imprints of animals and plants preserved in rock.

FRACTURE
A break in a mineral or rock that is not related to its atomic structure.

FRONT
Area where two different air masses collide.

GEYSER
A fountain of hot water or steam heated by volcanic activity.

GLACIER
Mass of ice on land that flows downhill under its own weight.

GLOBAL WARMING (GREENHOUSE EFFECT)
An increase in the global temperature as a result of heat being trapped in the atmosphere by gases such as carbon dioxide.

GRANITE
A coarse-grained intrusive igneous rock.

GUYOT
Flat-topped submarine (undersea) mountain.

HABITAT
The environment in which an animal or plant lives.

HIGH
An area of high atmospheric pressure

HOARFROST
Water vapor from fog that crystallizes as ice on rough, cold surfaces.

HURRICANE
Violent tropical storm, with high winds and torrential rain.

IGNEOUS ROCK
Rock formed when magma or lava solidifies.

INTRUSIVE IGNEOUS ROCK
Rocks resulting from injection of lava into existing rocks.

ISOBAR
Line on a weather chart joining points with equal air pressure.

LAVA
Magma erupted from fissures and volcanoes.

LIGNITE
Soft, woody coal formed by the burial of peat.

LIMESTONE
Sedimentary rock, mostly calcium carbonate.

LITHOSPHERE
The outer layer of the Earth which contains the crust and upper part of the mantle.

LONGSHORE DRIFT
The movement of sand and sediment along a beach by waves moving obliquely to the shore.

LOW
An area of low atmospheric pressure.

MAGMA
Molten rock material under the Earth's surface.

MANTLE
The thick layer between the core and the crust of the Earth.

MARBLE
A metamorphic rock, formed when limestone or another carbonate rock is changed by heat and/or pressure.

MERCALLI SCALE
A 12-step scale that rates an earthquake by its destructiveness.

METAMORPHIC ROCK
Rock formed by the effect of pressure and heat on existing rock.

METEOROLOGY
The scientific study of weather.

MIDOCEANIC RIDGE
The huge mountain range that runs through all ocean basins.

MINERAL
A naturally occurring substance with a constant chemical composition

ORBIT
The path taken by a planet as it travels around the Sun, or by a moon or spacecraft, which travels around a planet.

ORE MINERAL
Mineral that contains enough metal or nonmetal to make its removal profitable.

OZONE LAYER
Layer in the upper atmosphere containing ozone, a gas that absorbs the Sun's ultraviolet rays

PALEONTOLOGY
Scientific study of fossils.

PEAT
Dark soil formed by the partial decomposition of vegetation in wet areas of marsh or swamp.

PERMEABLE ROCK
Rock that allows water and other liquids, such as oil, to pass through it.

PLATE TECTONICS
A theory suggesting the lithosphere is made of rigid plates that move relative to each other.

POLLUTION
Gases, liquids, or solids,
largely released ir
deposited by humans,
that contaminate the
environment.

PRECIPITATION
Rain, sleet, hail, and
snow that fall to the
ground from clouds.

PREVAILING WIND
The usual or common
wind direction for an area.

RAINBOW
Colored arc seen in the
sky, formed when
sunlight splits into the
colors of the spectrum.

**REGIONAL
METAMORPHISM**
Large-scale change of rock
that results from plate
collision and mountain
building.

RICHTER SCALE
A measure of earthquake
energy based on the
amplitude of surface waves
recorded on seismographs.

RIFT (GRABEN)
Sinking of a strip of the
lithosphere between two
faults.

ROCK
Solid mass made of one
or more minerals.

SAVANNA
Grassland area at the
edge of the tropics,
which has seasonal rain.

SCREE
Mass of boulders and
smaller fragments that
accumulate at the
bottom of cliffs and
mountain slopes.

SEISMIC WAVE
A shock wave from an
earthquake, measured
using a seismometer.

SEISMOLOGY
The study of earthquakes
and earth structure.

SMOG
A mixture of smoke
and fog.

SOLAR SYSTEM
The Sun and the planets,
meteors, comets, moons,
and asteroids orbiting
the Sun.

SPREADING RIDGE
Submarine mountains
where two plates are
moving apart and new
crust is being created.

STALACTITE
Conical mineral deposit
hanging from a cave roof.

STALAGMITE
Conical mineral deposit
that builds up from the
cave floor.

STRATUS CLOUD
Low-lying, layered cloud.

STREAK
The color of a mineral in
its powdered form.

SUBDUCTION ZONE
Plane along which
oceanic lithosphere sinks
beneath an opposing
plate.

TORNADO
Violent thunderstorm
producing a destructive
funnel cloud underneath.

TRADE WINDS
Winds that blow from
high-pressure regions of
subtropical belts toward
areas of low pressure at
the equator.

TSUNAMI
Destructive sea waves
caused by earthquakes
under the ocean.

VOLCANO
A vent in the lithosphere
through which magma
erupts as lava.

WEATHER
Atmospheric conditions
at a particular time and
place.

WEATHERING
Physical and chemical
processes that break
down rocks on the
Earth's surface.

Index

Acknowledgments

Dorling Kindersley would like to thank:
DK Cartography for the maps, Hilary Bird for the index, and Robert Graham and Connie Mersel for editorial assistance.

Photographs by:
J. Stevenson, C. Keates, A. von Einsiedel, H. Taylor, A. Crawford, G. Kevin, D. King, S. Shott, K. Shone.

Illustrations by:
J. Temperton, J. Woodcock, N. Hall, R. Ward, E. Fleury, B. Donohoe, D. Wright, C. Salmon, B. Delf, P. Williams, S. Quigley, R. Shackell, R. Lindsay, P. Bull, P. Visscher, R. Blakeley, R. Lewis, L. Corbella, D. Woodward, C. Rose, N. Loates, G. Tomlin.

Picture credits: t=top b=bottom c=center l=left r=right
AKG London: Erich Lessing / Galleria dell'Accademia 68bl. Bridgeman Art Library: British Museum 77bl; Christie's, London 48-49t. British Coal: 79tl. British Crown: 72tr. Bruce Coleman: G. Cubitt 77br; A. Davies 55bl, br; Dr. M. P. Kahl 149cl; H. Lange 74-75; W Lawler 144t; Dr. John MacKinnon 148tr; M. Timothy O'Keefe 83b; Fritz Prenzel 57tl; Andy Purcell 139tr; Gunter Ziesler 148br. Ecoscene: A. Brown 52tl, 139br, 142-143; R. Glover 136bc; Pat Groves 119t; Sally Morgan 52bl, 62tr; Tweedie 68tl; P. Ward 146br. Mary Evans Picture Library: 32bl, 44c. Frank Lane Picture Agency: 36bl,

H. Hoslinger 141c; S. Jonasson 41cl; S. McCutcheon 42-43, 49bl; National Park Service 30-31. GeoScience Features Picture Library: 36tl, 39tr. Robert Harding Picture Library: 50-51, 63tl, 93tl; D. Hughes 90tl; Krafft 38br; R. Rainford 86tl. Hulton Deutsch Collection: 77tl, 99bl, 124b, 134tr. Image Bank: 86bl, 88br; L. Brown 126-127; G. Champlong 122t; T. Madison 61tl; B. Rou 137c. Mountain Camera: J. Cleare 32tl. NASA: 10-11, 140tr. National History Museum: 65bc, 66cl, 67bl. Oxford Scientific Films: Ben Osborne 146bl. Planet Earth: J. Downer 124t; J. Fawcett 40tl; R. Hessler 41 C. Huxley 2tr, 102-103; J. Lithgoe 98tr; J. Merdsoy 94-95; W. M. Smithey 93bl; N. Ta 90bl. Rex Features: A. Fernandez 37t; SIPA Press 46tl. Science Museum, London: 149b Science Photo Library: D. Allan 92t; Tony Craddock 84-85; Dan Farber 140br; S. Frase 139bl; J. Heseltine 54tl; D. Pellegrini 100tr; Dr. Morley Read 146tl; NASA 112; F. Sauz 106tr; US Geological Survey 22-23. Solarfilma: 38tr. Frank Spooner Pictures: Barr/Liaison 36br; Garties/LN 39tl; Vitti/Gamma Liaison. Tony Stone Images: 60t, 62br, 80tr, 82tr; T. Braise 125b. Tony Waltham: 32cl, 34tl, 116-117. L. White, 118t. Zefa: 48br, 88cl, 138t, 147tc.

Every effort has been made to trace the copyright holders and we apologize in advance for any unintentional omissions. We would be pleased insert the appropriate acknowledgments in any subsequent edition of this publication.

Critical acclaim for Peter Robinson
and the Inspector Banks series

'The Alan Banks mystery-suspense novels
are the best series on the market. Try one
and tell me I'm wrong'
Stephen King

2

'A powerfully moving work'
Ian Rankin

'Top-notch police procedure'
Jeffery Deaver

'A wonderful novel'
Michael Connelly

'An addictive crime-novel series'
New York Times

'A guaranteed page-turner'
Mirror

'It demonstrates how the crime novel,
when done right, can reach parts that other
books can't . . . A considerable achievement'
Guardian

'One of the most authentic and
atmosph

'The master of the police procedural'
Mail on Sunday

'Near, perhaps even at the top of,
the British crime writers' league'
The Times

'Banks is genuinely human,
rather than a hard man'
Observer

'Peter Robinson emerges as a definite
contender for fiction's new top cop'
Independent on Sunday

'Absorbing'
Scotsman

'Atmospheric'
Time Out

'Exhilarating'
Toronto Star

'Peter Robinson is a mystery writer's
mystery writer . . . I can't imagine a
more flawless police procedural'
Globe and Mail – Canada